8
VIRTUES
OF RAPIDLY
GROWING
CHURCHES

Matt Miofsky
& Jason Byassee

FOREWORD BY JACOB ARMSTRONG

VIRTUES
OF RAPIDLY
GROWING
CHURCHES

Abingdon Press™

Nashville

EIGHT VIRTUES OF RAPIDLY GROWING CHURCHES

Library of Congress Cataloging-in-Publication Data has been requested.

ISBN 978-1-5018-5273-2

18 19 20 21 22 23 24 25 26 27—10 9 8 7 6 5 4 3 2 1
MANUFACTURED IN THE UNITED STATES OF AMERICA

From Jason: for Craig and Trygve

and

From Matt: for the people of
First Washington United Methodist Church

CONTENTS

ACKNOWLEDGMENTS

I am grateful first of all to my co-author, Matt Miofsky, planter and pastor of one of the most interesting churches we have in Methodism, or anywhere for that matter. This book was an excuse to get to know and to learn from Matt. Most of the good ideas are his. I wrote some of the good sentences. Pushing on one another's prose at the Eden Seminary library, meeting one another's families, watching baseball in St. Louis and Vancouver, and hosting him to preach at Tenth Church and teach at the Vancouver School of Theology have all been a gift. Thanks Matt. Thanks to Jaylynn for triaging the homefront while I traveled to St. Louis, Atlanta, Sioux Falls and Nashville; and to Jessica for doing the same as Matt traveled in his explorations.

We are grateful to our interview subjects. Ridiculously busy people all, they nevertheless made time for us, were patient with our stupidest questions, bore their souls and got nothing in return except the risk of being misquoted. I hope this book honors them and their extraordinary ministries.

I am grateful to Bill Gattis, retired pastor from the North Carolina Conference of the UMC, who invited me and Matt to the (now defunct!) North Carolina Festival of Homiletics. We met there and back-of-the-napkinned what became this book. Bill pastored me and my mother at University United Methodist in Chapel Hill back when she dragged me to church once or twice a year. She was not an easy person to pastor—as he learned! I was delighted, but not surprised, to learn of his kind pastoral care for her years after her death. God bless every act of pastoral tenderness on the planet, most of which go unnoticed by anyone other than the recipient and God. And pastors: pay attention to those who only turn up occasionally. They might be back for more later. Much more.

Thanks also to David Teel and Connie Stella at Abingdon for bringing it to an audience and to Laurie Vaughen for her editing help. Thanks to the Vancouver School of Theology, where I teach preaching for my day job, and to First Baptist Church of Vancouver, where I served an interim stint in the fall of 2018.

This book is dedicated to two friends who are campus ministers: Craig Kocher and Trygve Johnson. I give thanks on behalf of the students and faculty and staff of the University of Richmond and of Hope College, blessed as they are to have these two as chaplains. A campus minister has to replant a church every year in a sense, as leaders graduate and new people turn up. They have to hone their skills constantly since that new cohort has fresh assumptions and newly mystifying instincts. This is why campus ministers are some of our best pastors, and these two are among the best I'll ever know. I met because of the two of them—Craig spotted Trygve's ministry at Hope and encouraged me to go visit. I give thanks for two of my closest friends and hope they and all campus ministers are blessed by this book.

Jason Byassee

I am grateful to my co-author Jason Byassee. He will often say that I had all the good ideas. That is not true, and there wouldn't be a book without him. He is the one that conceived of the idea for the book and pushed me to start writing. He is not only a brilliant writer and thinker, but an excellent pastor. I am grateful for his guidance and leadership throughout this project.

I am grateful to the pastors that we interviewed, most of whom are friends of mine. Talking with Jacob, Laura, Scott, Jorge, Olu, and Adam taught me a lot and inspired my own work here at The Gathering. People will tell you the church is dying. Talking with leaders like these will confirm that it isn't!

I am grateful to my wife Jessica and my kids—Caleb, Carly, and George. They give up a lot of time with me so that I can work on projects like this. I am grateful to Jaylynn and Jason's own family, as I know they do the same. Our ministries truly are shared endeavors.

I am grateful to my friend Mike Wondel who has not only been one of my closest friends in ministry but served as a sounding board for many of the ideas that made it in this book. Processing out loud with him helped clarify my own thoughts. I am grateful to many of the pastors around the country who gave me critical feedback on these ideas as I shared and taught them. These pastors served churches large and small, urban and rural, conservation and liberal, predominantly white and predominantly people of color. The contributions and insights they offered made the ideas in this book sharper, the insights more broadly applicable, and the book better.

Thank you to David, Laurie, and Connie at Abingdon for their faith in the project, advice along the way, and work in getting these virtues to a wider audience.

Finally, I am grateful to The Gathering—the people, the leaders, and the staff who have taught me so much about what a compelling ministry looks like. I get far too much credit for the growth of our church, and they get far too little. The church has done so much for me, including giving me the time and space to write this book. I am especially indebted to my assistant, Amy Sanders. This book would not have even gotten off the ground without her.

I want to dedicate this book to the people of First Washington United Methodist Church. This is the church that raised me and first taught me why compelling ministry matters. They introduced me to Jesus and provided the foundation for my love of ministry and deep belief in the power of a local church.

Matt Miofsky

FOREWORD

I have for years followed the ministries of Matt Miofsky and Jason Byassee. Like you, I listen closely when I hear them speak at conferences and I set aside time to read their latest books and posts. They are both bright, engaging, and have something to say about the people of God in a time such as this. But, I follow them closely because they also care. They care about the church. They care about injustice. They care about people. Unlike a lot of us in the church today in America, they haven't given up. They struggle with and pray through the difficult things the church is facing, and they do it with care and with hope.

I have long considered Matt, one of my dear friends, a deep-thinking theological genius operating under the guise of a local church pastor. Matt continually talks about his call as a local church pastor to a particular context, and yet it is abundantly clear that God has also given his voice to a much wider audience. Matt is able to articulate complex theological concepts and how to live them out in the church in plain and simple ways. He is a big help to practitioners like me. Matt's voice is a breath of fresh air to those of us who practically want to know how to be better pastors, leaders, and Christians.

For years, I only knew Jason from afar. I read his articles in national publications and saw him engage in scholarly debate. After growing to know him more, I have learned that I had him stereotyped. He is for sure a deep-thinking theological genius, but underneath that is the heart and the calling of a pastor. He isn't just concerned with high and lofty conversation; he desperately wants to see how our thinking can inform our Christian living.

So, I was thrilled to hear that pastor/theologian Matt and theologian/pastor Jason were writing a book. I knew they would make accessible things that many of us have been trying to mine for some time.

They called to ask me some questions about my church for the book. Their last question surprised me. All the others were predictable. Their initial questions concerned discipleship systems, growth patterns, and best practices. As the interview came to a close though, their last question caught my attention and I still think of it often. First, it began with a big disclaimer. The question I was told was strange, out of the ordinary, and I didn't have to answer it if it didn't make sense. It was as if they didn't want to presuppose something or impose anything on me, but still they had to ask. My curiosity was piqued; it reminded me of when one of my daughters is trying to make some grand request like asking for her whole class to have a sleepover at our house or to get a zoo animal for Christmas. She knows I will say no, but she just has to ask.

Matt and Jason's question: "Did we experience any miracles in the early days of our church forming?"

Miracles. That's a word I don't often hear. And as a pastor of a church that has grown quickly, I'd have to say it was the first time anyone outside of our church ever asked me about my belief or the presence of miracles.

"Yes," I said. "I believe in and we have experienced miracles."

My mind was flooded with images from our church's nine-year history. I first saw in my mind's eye a high school student walking down the center aisle of our worship service with the help of a walker. A few months before I had stood in the ICU of the trauma unit at Vanderbilt Hospital when the words "he will never walk again" were uttered by a doctor. I was asked by his dad to anoint his son and pray for him. Having no oil in my pocket, I took water from the sink and put it on his head in the sign of a cross and prayed for his healing. Nothing happened. But then, a few months later I was surprised mid-sermon by Doug walking down the aisle. Our congregation stood and applauded as we had all been praying for him. We had been pleading for him. It sounds like something that happens in an arena, staged by a slick healer-preacher man. This, though, happened in an elementary school gym with a couple hundred people who were trying to believe we were a church. That day we became a church that believed God could do anything.

I remembered how we acquired the land where our church now sits. It was the last piece of residential land in the development where we were starting a church. We bought it for $1 million less than the original asking price. "Why?" we asked the old land owner. He said he believed "in the dream God had given us."

When Jason and Matt asked me the miracle question I remembered miracle after miracle that can't be explained by natural reasons. I had never thought about it before, but our church was built on miracles. We had studied Acts 2 over and over again. Our small group ministry, the building blocks of our church, is based on Acts 2:42. Everybody knows it. But I had missed verse 43 that says the church was filled with signs and wonders.

So, I shouldn't have been surprised to see this book starts with that virtue. The virtue of a miraculous God. You will read quickly that it isn't just the churches discussed in this book that experience God's presence and power in miraculous ways. But, these churches are looking for them everywhere. Perhaps this book will lead the church to look for miracles again.

When I shared with my leadership team the findings of this book, we discussed them in detail. A few of the virtues caused us to nod our heads as we read them, a few caused some more conversation, and a couple of them caused us to stop. To stop and realize we needed to realign, once again. One virtue stopped us in our tracks. Something that at one time we felt like we were doing really well is now something we had almost forgotten. We talked in practical terms about how we could re-engage it.

But after my team spent an hour or so on the 8 virtues, we were led to pray. We prayed like we hadn't in a long time. In a living room in a circle we prayed long and deep. We shed tears. We felt God's spirit. We felt hope for the future.

You will find this a very practical book. You should read it with your church leaders. You will get to learn from a pastor/theologian and a theologian/pastor who I consider to be two voices desperately needed in the church today.

But be warned, this book will lead you to pray. It will lead you to pray for new people to know Christ. It will lead you to pray for ways to bring good news to the poor. It will lead you to pray for miracles. It will give you eyes to see them. It will give you hope for the future of the church. It will give you hope for your church. Get ready—this is a great book.

Jacob Armstrong

WE CAN ALL LEARN FROM CHURCH PLANTERS

A church is not a recipe or a template or a blueprint. It is a mystery. A participant in the mystery of the resurrected and living Christ. We disgrace a mystery when we treat it like a formula to be copied. Instead we should stand in awe of a mystery: admire it, ponder what we stand to learn about God from it, speak about it to others. We hope this book, with its profiles of highly successful church plants, provides rich fodder for your pondering, examples for you to learn from.

There is a right way to learn from other churches and church plants. And there are multiple wrong ways. Wrong ways first—they're easier.

First, don't try to copy or replicate exactly what you admire in the churches you read about here. Don't treat these profiles as formulas, or as easily repeatable procedures that can work in any time and place. Avoid the temptation to think that if you copy what's done by these churches, you too can have a successful church, envied by your peers, admired at conferences, maybe even linked to a book deal. Don't get me wrong—there is plenty to learn here, or we wouldn't have written this book. But we should borrow—not copy—from whatever source we can in our efforts to be faithful. No two flourishing churches will be just alike.

Another wrong way to learn would be to be dismissive. *Pshaw—that can't happen here.* Churches often have long memories of experimentation that ended badly, leaving the congregation to opine forever, "We tried that. It doesn't work." There is something right about this skepticism. As we know from the "wrong way" above, not everything will work in every place. Maybe there are some places where nothing will "work." But there is never nothing to be learned. Especially from churches as innovative, creative, and fruitful as the ones we highlight in this book.

What is the right way to learn? Well, in a sense, we are *all* church planters now. There may have been a day when pastors came out of seminary and started on the pastoral career ladder from associate to small church as a solo pastor to being in charge of multi-staff at a tall steeple. There may have been a day when any batch of people could throw open any set of doors, set out a sandwich board, and folks would flock. But now every church is under duress—the big ones included. Folks don't just automatically come to church in North America anymore. Children of our most faithful people don't worship God corporately anymore or don't with us, and their children often have no experience of church at all, even to rebel against. We have all heard this story of secularization in America, and there can be some good things about it. Equating citizenship with church-going was probably always a bad idea, though it was hard to see that when things were flush. They're not now. Every church is about ten minutes away from closing. And that's good. Nothing is immortal except God alone. Churches, like people, come to life in a rush, grow awkwardly, plateau into middle age, and decline—there's a natural life cycle to such things. A gracious closing is far better than raging against the inevitable. Our system as Methodists has often been really good at keeping dying churches from closing and keeping growing churches from growing more.

But there is grace in all of this. All of us have the opportunity to plant something new in soil fertilized by dead and decaying things. It's smelly, gross, and difficult work. But something beautiful can grow. In fact, that's the natural way of things. Healthy things grow. All the more so with the gospel. God seems to delight in upending the "natural" life cycle in the Bible—ninety-year-olds have babies, battlefields strewn with bones stand up right and put on flesh again, people on the far side of death are summoned back to life by a word from Jesus, hapless Romans post guards at tombs and still can't stop resurrection. The good news of God restoring the cosmos through Jesus Christ should fall on glad ears. The church should be naturally compelling, even in times of post-Christendom. Churches like those profiled here can help show us how to garden amidst difficulty, but with delight.

The churches with which we started our research were among the handful that were then the fastest growing congregations in Methodism in America. We focused on Methodism because it is our tribe. The book could have been indefinitely expanded by including other Protestant denominations (for complicated reasons Catholics and Orthodox don't use the same language or model of "planting" as churches of the Reformation). Our evangelical colleagues have spoken of and taken up planting longer and more avidly than we have. Yet among mainline liberal denominations Methodists, at least for now, have the warmest relationships to evangelicals. We don't mind borrowing from them, and so can show other denominations how to do likewise. We are also not a dogmatically driven church. Some Reformed and Baptist churches that have been plenty invested in church planting have heavy dogmatic statements that must be agreed to in advance before a congregation qualifies as properly "church." We have dogma as Methodists, and robust debates about how important it is and in what way precisely. But we tend to under-emphasize it, for better or worse. We were born as a revivalist renewal movement within our mother church, the Church of England, so at our best we combine emphases that are evangelical, sacramental, and activist in favor of social justice. At our worst we can just be fuzzy and unclear. We hope this book emphasizes our best face: confident in the gospel and open to others.

These churches exhibit a remarkable diversity. Some are in down-town urban cores (Church of the Resurrection Downtown in Kansas City, Missouri). Others are in large urban areas but not within the walkable downtowns (Impact in Atlanta, The Gathering in St. Louis, and Providence in Nashville). Two are in mid-size cities that are grow-ing (Grace Church in Cape Coral, Florida, and Embrace Church in Sioux Falls, South Dakota). One is in a far-flung exurb that until ten minutes ago was a rural farming community—Bee Creek Methodist in Spicewood, Texas, outside Austin. These churches are pastored by people who are young and old, male and female, and from a variety of racial and ethnic backgrounds. They are not, in other words, all hipsters in skinny jeans with ironic facial hair and a thing for smoke machines. They are ordinary pastors with seminary degrees from a variety of institutions from liberal to evangelical, from Methodist to everything-else. They don't all fit the "most likely to succeed" de-mographic, though it wouldn't surprise you to see them succeed in whatever endeavor they choose. They're just surprisingly ordinary. Again don't get us wrong. They are brilliant! But they are not su-perhuman. They are more eager to share mistakes than successes. They are slightly baffled by all that has "worked" on their watch. We noticed similarities as we talked with them. Patterns. Not recipes. Similar trends that "work" to some degree across space and time, with significant outliers that we will note. One common pattern is that these patterns are all worthy of our admiration, respect, and love. They are the best of our tradition and of any Christian tradition. They're the sort you want at your bedside while dying, at the delivery room while giving birth, at the pulpit on Sunday, at the board meeting proposing a new initiative. There is a reason their churches are growing—and they are part of that reason.

But they are not the only reason. There is a mystery to churches that grow. Some good and faithful pastors do their best, and things come unglued. Some (though this is less common) poor pastors are just in the right place at the right time, and things grow. Not all growth is healthy. Tumors grow—sometimes fast. Epidemics and scandals too. Churches that grow aren't ipso facto faithful, and churches that are faithful don't ipso facto grow.

But Methodism is a revivalist movement. If we, of all God's church, are not *reviving anybody*, then what are we there for?! Other churches may have the constitution to be satisfied with maintenance. Not us. There is a complex history behind why and how Methodism went from sawdust trails and backwoods revivals into downtown corner buildings with tall steeples and gothic architecture and endowments. All of it can be a defense against the living God. And God can use all of it. God has used churches and pastors as diverse as these to communicate the gospel to those who haven't heard, to feed the hungry, to bless their communities, in short, to embody the new creation Christ is bringing. We wrote this book in the hopes that it will help your church do more of the same. May God make it so for all of us.

VIRTUE #1

RAPIDLY GROWING CHURCHES BELIEVE IN MIRACLES AND ACT ACCORDINGLY

Rapidly growing churches experience early miracles in which the Spirit shows up in surprising, unexpected, game-changing ways. As a result, these churches begin to look for miracles, expect them, and operate as if God's power to do the unexpected is real.

This book started with a pretty simple premise. In the midst of a culture where so many churches are in decline, why do certain churches grow, and grow rapidly? Something is happening here, and it is out of the ordinary. So why? I (Matt) get asked that question all the time. In the middle of a city (St. Louis) that is experiencing population loss, economic challenges, social upheaval, and deteriorating churches, why is The Gathering growing? Since I get asked it so much, I have had a lot of time to think about the answer. Want to hear it?

The Gathering is growing because the Spirit is doing something new and beautiful in St. Louis. We as a church spend most of our time trying to ride that wave without falling off. The Spirit is up to

1

something miraculous, and we believe in that so much that we operate as if it is true, day in and day out.

Now I know that answer might sound trite to some of you. I can hear it now: "Yes, yes, the Spirit. We know it's God. But tell us about your worship, your small groups, your mission work…" This is what we do. We skip over the best part, the only real way the church grows. We skip over the miracle-producing work of the Holy Spirit. And I think I know why.

When we started talking to pastors of rapidly growing churches and hearing their stories, we began to notice a pattern. Somewhere, at some point, these churches experienced things that most churches only dream about. A gift of land that is given to a church needing a permanent home. A leading area musician walking through the doors of a church that has been praying for better worship music. A highly qualified, bright, passionate, talented, and faithful person gives up their well-paying full-time job to commit their energy to the church. The area newspaper does a major story at just the right time; we could keep going. But the point is this: at some early stage, these churches had a miracle in which the Holy Spirit showed up in a surprising, unexpected, game-changing way.

When I share this observation with other pastors, the initial reaction is often exasperation. After all, we cannot manufacture miracles. We can pray, sure. We can hope. But we can't *make* miracles happen. If church growth is dependent on the surprising, miracle-producing work of the Holy Spirit, then that leaves us pretty helpless. Or so we might think. In fact, that is what we thought. We almost left this first chapter out precisely because we wanted to share observations that people could use, that were transferable, that could work in any setting. But as you know, the Spirit blows and we know not where it comes from or where it goes.

But then something happened. I started thinking more about these miracle stories from rapidly growing churches. I started to reflect on miracles I have experienced at The Gathering. I started talking to pastor friends whose churches may not be on the fast-growing list, but nonetheless could name miracles that God was doing in their own midst, and I discovered that this idea does not leave us helpless. What I discovered is that miracles are actually happening everywhere. In small towns and big cities, in wealthy churches and poor ones. In multisite megachurches and in rural four-point charges. Miracles are happening. Here is the difference—some churches (and church leaders) live and work and act like they *believe* this, and others don't. This distinction makes all the difference.

Acting as if we believe that the Holy Spirit is up to something in our midst is the single greatest game-changing decision a church leadership team can make. Talk to any of the pastors we interviewed and you will instantly see that before there was any evidence that a church would work, these pastors believed that God was up to something, that God was going to do something significant. They were determined to be a part of it. Acting as if the Spirit is moving changes everything.

For starters, we discovered that churches that believe in the miraculous movement of the Holy Spirit pray fervently, specifically, and boldly. Jorge Acevedo tells a story that occurred shortly after he was appointed to Grace Church, at the time a traditional United Methodist Church in Florida. He had a strong belief that God was going to use the church to reach people who were disconnected from Christ. To do this, he decided to start a contemporary worship service (at the time a risky and controversial step). The morning of the first service came, and he was standing in the new space when someone said to him, "It'll never work." He was launching a contemporary service in a traditional place. But he spent that early morning praying over every chair, over every new person who would come, and praying that the Holy Spirit would produce a miracle. He went back into his office to prepare for worship. When he came out, 261 people were gathered for worship. He describes it as his Pentecost moment. More important than the number, though, was the habit. They were going to pray for the Holy Spirit to work, expect that the Spirit would work, and prepare for the miracles that the Spirit wanted to do in their midst.

Now I know what some of you are thinking. Not every prayer is answered in such a way. We all pray. Maybe you've prayed just this kind of prayer, except no one new showed up. An early morning prayer does not necessarily correspond to hundreds of new people. In fact, it rarely does. But prayer does something else that matters. Praying fervently, boldly, and specifically for miracles begins to focus our vision. It helps us to be on the lookout for where God might be working—and where we were perhaps missing God.

Olu Brown at Impact Church in Atlanta tells a story about early leaders in his church. As many of you know, when you are trying to get something new going in your church, you often pray that God would send a seasoned, mature, thoughtful, and committed church person through your doors. You know, someone who can lead, who tithes, who isn't dysfunctional, and who actually shows up to worship, even when it rains. Early on, Olu received a few people just like that, and he was so thankful. But there was a problem. They would stay for a season, but then for one reason or another, they would move, switch churches, or pass away. At first, Olu shared his frustration at "losing" good people. But then he began to see it differently. He realized that each of these leaders miraculously showed up at Impact, helped Impact through a critical early season with their unique gifts, and then left. He realized that God was sending angels to help them through vulnerable early stages of starting a new church. So instead of focusing

4

on who he was losing, he began looking for the next person that God would send through the doors. Every new person became a potential angel, there to serve a key role in what God was doing. Belief in the Spirit and prayer changed how he saw each person he met.

This virtue matters because when we believe that God is up to something even in our context, we pray differently, we see differently, and most importantly we begin to act differently. This is perhaps why this virtue matters so much. In the rapidly growing churches we studied, a belief in the miracle-producing work of the Spirit led such churches to not only pray, to not only see, but ultimately to act. They are churches that consistently make big bets and bold moves that other churches are afraid to make because they believe the Spirit is at work. The Spirit prompts them to act more boldly. And if you want to get results that most churches don't get, you have to be willing to make decisions that most churches won't make.

Most of us know the story of Moses splitting the Red Sea with his staff. It is told in Exodus 14. The Israelites had fled Egypt with the tacit permission of Pharaoh. As they fled, they camped down for the night on the shores of the red sea. Suddenly Pharaoh changed his mind. He ordered his army to chase after Moses. Soon the Israelites found themselves trapped in an impossible situation. On one side was a vast sea. On the other side was the army of Pharaoh racing toward them. They were no match for the army, and they had no way to cross the sea. The situation was about as hopeless as it could get. And so they turned to Moses, and said

> Weren't there enough graves in Egypt that you took us away to die in the desert? What have you done to us by bringing us out of Egypt like this? Didn't we tell you the same thing in Egypt? "Leave us alone! Let us work for the Egyptians!" It would have been better for us to work for the Egyptians than to die in the desert. (Exod 14:10-12)

5

Have you ever heard a version of this before? You want to do something risky, you want to try something new, you want to go for a bold initiative but the task feels impossible—like being stuck between a massive army and a raging sea. And it seems like there is no way forward. Worse than that, the very people you lead seem content to sit tight and die where they are—rather than trying something new. Moses pleads with them to trust God, pleads with them to keep moving forward. But they won't. They are frozen on the shore.

Most of us know what happens next. Moses stretches out his arm and God splits the sea, making a way where there was no way. We know that part of the story. But you may not know a little detail that made its way into the Jewish rabbinical tradition. According to the midrash, there was one more thing that was needed before God would split the sea and show the way forward. Someone had to brave enough to wade out into the swirling water. Someone had to be willing to walk out into the sea *before* God would do the miracle. That person was a man named Nahshon. According to tradition, Nahshon walked out into the roaring water. But he didn't stop when the water hit his ankles, or his knees, or even his waist. He had to wade all the way out until it was at his neck and threatening to drown him. Then, and only then, did God begin to part the waters.

There are a lot of lessons in this little piece of Jewish midrash. But one of them is this. We have to act boldly. We have to act as if we expect God to do miracles. We have to try things that, if God is not real, will almost certainly fail. The more boldly we act, the more likely we are to see miracles happening. After all, as long as the people stood safely on the shore, the sea remained an impassable obstacle. It was only when one person was willing to go, trusting that God would do something miraculous, that the impossible occurred.

6

So who are you? Who is your church? Will you be one of the thousand on the shore, or the one who steps out believing that a miracle is possible?

Churches Don't Close because They Risk Too Much

In talking with the leadership of rapidly growing churches, a similar principle seems to be at play. To put it simply, these churches are willing to try things that most churches are unwilling to try in order to get results that most churches don't.

Jorge Acevedo tells a story about one of his riskiest early decisions at Grace Church. After stepping out and starting a contemporary worship service alongside the church's long-standing traditional service, they saw the new service grow while the traditional service did not. As the contemporary service filled up, they knew that a second one would be needed. It made the most sense to do it at 11:00 a.m., the time of the traditional service. A solution was emerging: they would change the traditional service to a second contemporary service. So Jorge decided to use all the "trust chips" that he had accumulated and told the traditional folks that the format of the service was going to change. It was a risky move. Immediately they lost eighty people, many of whom were long-time attenders and financial givers. The remaining folks were skeptical. Parishioners again said it wouldn't work. Failure was a very real option. After a year, however, the service actually grew by 150 people. But it didn't happen without real moments of fear and trepidation. They had to watch eighty people leave before they began to see new people connecting and the church begin to grow. In retrospect, it looks like a great move, but during that period of decline, it took an enormous amount of courage and faith to keep going.

We share this story because it is so typical. Many of us have faced similar kinds of decisions. We see a ministry move that we think God is asking us to make, and yet by making it we risk alienating or angering a cohort of people at our church. Important people.

I (Matt) have the opportunity to travel and speak to churches that are seeking renewal and growth. In paying attention to the kinds of conversations I typically have with leaders, I have noticed two distinct patterns. Some church leaders will share with me their desire to reach new generations of people, engage more children, or reinvigorate their worship. I will start asking questions, and almost immediately they start sharing with me all the things that *can't* change: the worship style, the paint color, the Sunday school time, the worship committee chairperson, and so on. Whatever the circumstance, the outcome is the same. They aren't willing to make a hard, risk-taking move in order to do what they believe God is calling them to do. Instead they are looking for a solution that keeps people happy and maintains a roughly consensual stasis. They want to see the sea split without wading in up to their neck.

On the other hand, I will meet leaders who are ready and willing to rethink *everything* from the ground up in order to achieve a particular outcome. If it means changing a worship time, rethinking Sunday school, or dismantling the committee structure, they are willing to try it. You can guess which churches are in a better position to witness miracles and see different results: the ones that make bold decisions. The churches that can't or won't or choose to wait, even if the reasons are valid, usually don't.[1]

---

1. So we need to say that sometimes leaders change stuff unilaterally or otherwise unwisely. I have heard stories of churches changing worship styles or times or administrative structure dictatorially and then defending themselves by saying they were being bold.

Bold moves aren't just about a willingness to anger or even lose some people. This willingness extends to all areas of ministry, often with financial implications. Scott Chrostek tells a story about the risks associated with the purchase of Resurrection's first building downtown. They were a small community, eighty people, but felt that a permanent space was important for the church to demonstrate commitment to the city. An opportunity to buy a bar (next to a strip club) emerged. The provocative nature of the location aside, purchasing the building would require them to do a fast capital campaign, with eighty people, and all in about three weeks. They met, prayed, and decided to go for it. It had risk written all over it, but they knew they needed to do something, and they did. The decision paid off, and the site became their first permanent home, allowing them to establish credibility in the neighborhood and begin to grow as a church. The decision wasn't thoughtless, but it was financially risky and could have potentially set the church back if it didn't work. Failure was a real option, but the church saw an opportunity, felt God was calling, and made the move.

Contrast this with churches that consistently shepherd their finances to avoid disaster rather than to respond to the right opportunity when it arises. Let's be clear here. Responsibly managing a church's finances is faithful and important. This money was given in order to further a church's mission in a community. But when a church is in decline, they begin to make decisions differently. Often congregations are more afraid of running out of money than they are of missing a God-anointed possibility. But risky moves that are made in order to engage new people usually have financial implications. Churches have to be willing to rethink how they deploy their financial resources, and even risk losses, if they are going to truly change their trajectory. Playing it safe and maintaining a cautious course financially doesn't usually mesh well with a desire to try new things in order to get new results. We are not suggesting that you foolishly go all in with the church's finances. We are suggesting that an unwillingness to take risks financially will significantly restrain a church's ability to grow. It is hard to move forward when you are afraid of falling further behind.

Risky decisions can cost us people, they can cost us money, but they can also cost us something less tangible and visible. They can cost us emotional energy, confidence, and stress. Truly bold decisions contain within them the real possibility of failure. Most of us don't want to be the leaders responsible for a failing initiative. Even worse: What if we bet the farm and lose? It could accelerate the closure of an already fragile church. We are not pretending that these decisions don't come without real personal risk, anxiety, and even a loss of sleep. These kinds of decisions cost a leader something. Stepping into the water cost Nahshon something. We get to decide if that cost is worth it. But in churches where leaders are willing to withstand the cost of such moves, the payoff is often worth it. And many churches close with money still in the bank.

Don't Fear Failure

Olu Brown at Impact Church talks about the importance of not viewing failure negatively when leaders choose to try something risky. He recounts a time that his church decided to try a multi-site Easter worship service. One Easter weekend, they decided to include their main site and three additional off-site venues. The idea was risky, but they thought that the multisite approach would allow them to reach people who would not come to their permanent location. Easter morning arrived, and at one of the sites, no one showed up. Literally, no one! It was demoralizing, disappointing, and felt like a failure. (Olu reminded us it really was a failure.) As a leader, that hurts. That costs us something in the way of pride, confidence, and anxiety. These kinds of failures make us gun shy the next time around. Olu works hard, though, to deal with failure without assigning blame. Instead, at Impact, they celebrate the attempt, they learn from the experience, and most importantly, they encourage their leaders to keep trying.

Chances are some of you carry the scars of past bold moves that didn't pan out. We get it. It isn't easy. Oftentimes those failures leave our confidence in shambles and our credibility with the church depleted. We want to look as though we know what we are doing, and nothing erodes that sense more than an idea that didn't work. If you feel that way, then remember that your leaders and staff likely feel that way too. They have probably tried new things, made big bets, and risked new initiatives in the past only to watch such ministry get criticized or not work out. Maybe we have inadvertently sent signals to such leaders that failure is bad. Maybe we have outright critiqued failed ministry initiatives by others. Our churches can create an atmosphere where failure is punished (either overtly or subtly) or we can create a process of rewarding well-calculated risks and learning from failures all with an eye toward getting back up off the ground and trying again. Rapidly growing churches have figured out how to not only take risks but also deal with failure in a way that does not thwart future bold decisions. It is not an easy balance, but one that is characteristic of churches that grow.

At The Gathering we work hard to incentivize new ideas. In our ministry budget, we set aside a certain amount of money in a dream fund. This money is intended to fund creative, risky ideas that ministry staff want to try. They can pitch their ideas to the staff and well–thought-out, ministry-focused ideas can get funding that doesn't take away from their regular ministry budget. The finance team understands that the dream fund will not produce a winning idea every time. We certainly hope that it produces one or two a year, but we also know that failure is part of the process. But knowing that the money is meant to incentivize creativity and risk allows the team to relax when certain initiatives fail. Success for this fund does not mean every idea is a winner. Success means that staff regularly and enthusiastically are trying new things.

In our churches, we often overestimate the cost of trying something new and underestimate the cost of doing nothing. Fear holds us back from taking risks—fear of losing people, fear of losing money, fear of failing. What we don't often account for is the cost of not doing anything at all. I rarely hear a church fear not risking enough, fear not trying new ideas, or fear dying as a worshipping congregation with a million dollars still in the endowment. But these are the things we should fear. A friend of mine was chief risk officer for a major mission organization. His job was not just what you would expect—whether there would be risk in serving in this or that nation, and whether that risk was worth it. He was also charged to evaluate what the organization risked *by doing nothing.* What opportunities are present that will be gone if we delay and do nothing? If we just bury this talent safely in the ground, ready to be given back to its owner?

To return to our story, we don't know what was going through Nahshon's head. We might imagine how frightened he was. What was he thinking as the water hit his calves, his waist, his chest, his neck? Of course, he also could have been scared of not trying, of staying on the shore, of not getting to experience a miracle. That fear can slice both ways. The story ends with a healthy dose of hope.

Nahshon went for it, and as a result, all of Israel experienced a miracle. Nahshon was the first to walk across the sea on dry land. But it didn't come without a struggle. Walking out into the water, he knew full well he could be exposed as a fool, a naif, an idiot—just before all Israel died. Instead, his bravery was rewarded as the first one to step into God's new future.

When we believe in the miraculous work of the Spirit and try risky things in our own churches, the results will be no different. The hardest part of change is the time in between. One pastor describes it as sailing a ship far enough that you can no longer see the land you left, but not far enough to see the new place you are going. The Bible describes this as the wilderness, the place where you begin to doubt yourself and question the journey you are on. In the wilderness, the old way suddenly looks pretty good, you contemplate turning around, and you question whether God will really lead you anywhere new. When we are making bold moves, we are certainly going to experience these same emotions, and we will need Jesus' help along the way. Boldness and creativity aren't all on our shoulders. We don't have to figure it all out or come up with all the ideas. We do have to be willing to lead where the Spirit is nudging us, and we have to be willing to stand in that in-between time. When we start to falter, we have to stay connected to Jesus; and when we fail, we have to remember that our worth is not dependent on our track record. But ultimately, the cost of these decisions pales in comparison to the miracles we will experience when we adopt a more risk-taking posture in our church. We will experience the equivalent of stepping into the miraculuous freedom that God intends for all people.

If we want to experience miracles in our church, things that most churches don't get to experience, we have to be willing to try things that most churches are unwilling to try. Rapidly growing churches believe in miracles and act accordingly. They make big bets and bold moves that other churches are afraid to make. But one need not be rapidly growing to do the same. What we need is a willingness to believe and try, something we can all cultivate, no matter our context.

RAPIDLY GROWING CHURCHES INTEGRATE NEW PEOPLE QUICKLY

Superficial accounts of rapidly growing churches fixate on the person at the microphone. We all understand why this is. They're the easiest picture for the media. They're the person to whom nearly everybody present has to relate in some way. And they're really, really important. That person's ability to preach the gospel, to show its beauty to those most bored or skeptical, is crucial. It's hard to imagine a rapidly growing church without an excellent preacher.

But as they say in philosophy classes (are those still a thing?): excellent preaching is necessary, but not sufficient. Plenty of outstanding preachers have failed at church planting and leading. Church isn't just about getting people to show up one time or even lots of times. A professor of mine liked to say it's easy to get people in church: just set out a banner that says "Free beer!" and they'll fight each other for parking places. What you actually *do* with the people once they're in the building is what matters most, though.

Organize Discipleship, Not Bureaucracy

This truth is deep in Methodist DNA—so deep we hardly know it anymore. At the end of his remarkable life, George Whitefield stood back and found himself amazed at John Wesley's work. Wesley was not Whitefield's peer as a preacher. All hearers were clear Whitefield was the outstanding voice of that century. A skeptic no less than Benjamin Franklin used to say he would empty out every dollar in his pocket just upon hearing Whitefield say the word *Mesopotamia*. But looking at Wesley's Methodist societies, Whitefield compared his work to a "rope of sand." It looks solid, braided, secure, but try and pick it up, and it crumbles to dust in your hands. Wesley's societies spread the globe and their legacy remains to this day. The question is not whether the person at the front can get your attention with the word *Mesopotamia* or even can get you to empty out your wallet.

The question is, will they actually live a changed life?

Kind of Good

And here lots of our structure in Methodism is worse than un-helpful—it is actually harmful. There are layers upon layers of accumulated church junk in our congregations. Oceans of activities on which we spend legions of hours and rivers of ink in bulletins on things that are "kind of good," as Matt puts it. This or that sale, this or that study, this or that outing, this or that do-gooder endeavor. As one recent wag put it on social media, "Every dying church has a community garden." Ouch! (Every church I've served has had a community garden!) What we don't do is disciple people. That is, the very thing that once marked our movement. We were *called*

16

Methodists as others made fun of us: "You're so ridiculous! You think there's a method for holiness! Pray this prayer, fast this long, serve this day, invite others with you. Hah!" The Wesleys and others realized, "Wait, they're right, actually. We *do* think there are practices that by following you will grow in love of God and neighbor. Let's call ourselves that." And we did. We still do. But do we still do it? Do we still make disciples?

One thing rapidly growing churches (RGCs) do is they have a clear and effective discipleship process. Some call it connections, some assimilation, others new members orientation—but the purpose is the same—to help a new guest become a deeply committed follower of Christ. They make this discipleship process transparent for what they want people to do. User friendly, accessible, clear. They don't shower listeners with a thousand options for nice things they might do. They focus: do this, not that. They keep it simple, often linear. Start with this class. Next join a small group. Finally serve here. Think of the difference between sitting down and eating at the Cheesecake Factory, which famously boasts over 250 different menu options made from scratch, or eating at a cozy French bistro with a prix fixe menu. One offers a dizzying amount of choice; the other leads you through one carefully curated, skillfully crafted, and masterfully presented meal. RGCs act more like the prix fixe restaurant. They work on a simple, effective, and clear process that helps new people become disciples of Jesus. Everything and anything that takes away from that focus is cut. As Matt often puts it, rapidly growing churches are like ducks. They look placid on the water. But underneath they're paddling like crazy! The work is not so much in getting people in the door. It's in laying out for those people the next obvious steps to take in being a disciple.

Jorge Acevedo puts this point just as strongly. Once a church has its house in order, evangelism is easy: "The fish just jump in the boat. The gospel is good news, it sells itself, it's about what God does, not what we do," he said. "What we are beating our heads over is this question: How, once we connect people to Jesus, do we connect them to other followers of Jesus in order to grow?" Grace Church is launching a three-tier strategy for beginner, intermediate, and advanced growth. "It's not sexy," Jorge said. "But over against the cool backdrops and lights and skinny jeans, this is the thing. We're around a white board in a locked room begging God to help us make better disciples." Miofsky agrees. He says he knows no church that says they're just killing it in discipleship. Lots are doing well in mission or evangelism or preaching—you name it. But no one has this figured out. As he travels and speaks, it's the most common question he gets: "How do y'all do small groups?" Because as important as it is, it is not easy. But RGCs are constantly working on a better, clearer, and more effective discipleship process. It is a question that RGCs are constantly asking and never quite answering definitively.

One glaring example of the importance of prioritizing a simple and clear discipleship over "activity" is a project on which Grace has cut bait. They had a community center, modeled on Wesley's Foundry, through which Grace has given away 1.3 million pounds of food over seven years, to some 275,000 people. Most impressively, 1,000 of those have come to Christ in that time. That's an evangelistic bonanza! But when Grace looked around, they couldn't find 100 of those people in their church. So they're closing the ministry. Selling the building at a $1 million loss. Methodism isn't about community centers. We don't exist to give food away (though none of the ministries Grace was running through that center will die—they'll all be handed off to other, more appropriate organizations). We exist to make disciples. We can substitute that for other things that are "kind of good." But the Gospels warn sternly against substituting any other thing for the one thing that matters.

Acevedo reaches back into our heritage once again to illustrate this point—one he was willing to take a million-dollar hit to make. Wesley said it was better to leave a soul unstirred than to stir it and allow the evil one to snatch it away. Better for someone not to have heard and responded to the gospel than to respond and have no disciplined way of life to enter into in order for it to seep into the deepest pores, one's very way of being. Evangelism by itself is not Methodist. It is also necessary but not sufficient. Evangelism plus follow-up discipleship is what makes a church. Grace stays laser-focused on ministry with Sunday worship, on ministry with children, and on those in recovery. Everything else has to fall away.

Matt Miofsky also reaches back into our heritage, though on this side of the Atlantic. What made Francis Asbury the great evangelist he was is not that he preached to thousands of people in fields, important though that was. It was his messier, behind-the-scenes work of organizing, organizing, organizing. Asbury was not the most charismatic leader, to read his biographies. But he was a genius superintendent. His diaries attest this was all "really messy": "pastors quit all the time, people took off, he disciplined ineffective people, but he kept working at it." Over against the attention that charismatic people at microphones get (including in books like this one!), we over-value preaching and under-value order. We have to have systems to handle people. And in any church that looks like it has it all together, there are, behind the scenes, "people working hard, experimenting, who haven't figured it out." The Gathering in St. Louis has some 1,300 in worship attendance as of this writing and nearly 800 in core groups—a remarkable number. And a very, very Methodist one. The question in Methodism is not "When were you saved?"; it's "How are you growing in grace just now?"

Be Brave Enough to Say "No"

For Miofsky and The Gathering, simplifying the life and order of the church is crucial to disciple-making. In a rapidly growing church with lots of energy, folks will come with ideas about what more the church can do. These are often good things. But they aren't *the* thing. For The Gathering, the mission is "To invite new people to become deeply committed followers of Christ." And The Gathering disciplines itself to say no to anything—however appealing—that doesn't fit that narrow criterion. "It is a discipline about what to say yes to and what not to spend time and energy and resources on," Miofsky said. "We keep that tightly focused. That's harder to do the bigger you get."

One obvious example is in missions. What end could there be to the good things in the world a rapidly growing church like The Gathering could be doing? Early on the congregation narrowed to focus on education. This was an area in which St. Louis city schools really needed help, and The Gathering could focus its efforts and have an actual impact by saying no to all other possibilities, however tempting. When they asked city leaders what they really needed, they heard, again and again, help with education. They wanted folks to come in during the day to help kids read, mentor them, and encourage them. One large church could do that. So The Gathering took on a "ruthless focus" on education in the city. "The ugly side is," Miofsky cautions, "You will lose people who believe you need to be involved in their thing." That's where discipline comes in. We Methodists used to be known for that.

Embrace Church is the fastest growing among these fast-growing churches. And assimilation is what keeps Adam Weber up at night also. "It's easy to think this is all about Sunday and that's it," he said. "But we're working like crazy on the back end." Early on it's easy enough to tell who's new. As the preacher you walk up to them and talk to them personally. But worshipping with north of three thousand people in multiple sites, that is obviously impossible. "And we're failing miserably!" Weber insists, perhaps ungenerously to himself. One way forward is to notice which of the sites at the church is doing best at this. "It was our smallest place attendance-wise," Weber said. "But they're just killing it small-group-wise, because the pastor is dynamite: 'Hey, you're not in one? Oh my goodness, what are you doing?!' They're assimilating people like crazy." Weber is following here the time-honored technique of noticing where the Holy Spirit is working and then getting busy Copying And Stealing Everything (the CASE method) he can from that place.

Embrace has also done something similar to Grace Church— it's cut something that's a good thing, but not the best thing. As Jim Collins taught all of us, *good* is the enemy of *great*. It's just hard to back that up when it comes to programming. We assume if we put on as many programs as energetically as possible that they will all add up and compound themselves in ministry. But they won't. In Embrace's case, they had a plan set out to launch a day care in a community that needs it. This was a time-honored 1950s way for mainline churches to grow—get new families accustomed to the building, get kids agitating their parents to worship, grow the place. But it doesn't work now, if it ever did. Folks might assume that churches should be offering day care as a sort of public service.

They're willing to pay for it. But that willingness has relatively little connection to whether they'll turn up for worship. And it drains time and money and energy from the things the church absolutely has to be doing. "We said no to a preschool and no to day care too," Travis Waltner said of that decision. "Adam said, 'I want to reach more kids, but not through preschool.' Those projects would have made money even." Assimilating people as disciples has to be our primary focus. Every other focus, however laudable, has to lead to that end or be ruthlessly cut. As Olu Brown puts it about Impact's work in Atlanta, "We say 'here are two or three things we'll one day be great at.' Outside of those three, there are two or three other churches down the road happy to do what you want." We Methodists have been so anxious not to lose people that we don't want to say no to any good suggestion. So we never focus, we offer a dizzying pastiche of options no one can sort through, and we end up not doing one thing well. Ironically, we would do better in terms of not losing people, or at least gaining more, if we simplified, said no to more things, and said yes more strongly to fewer things.

"Our goal is not to be the coolest church," Jacob Armstrong says of Providence. "It's to reach people in the community in which we're placed." This required some adjustment of his internal barometer of success: "If I created the church I wanted as a twenty-seven-year old, it'd be great, with a few hundred people. And it would have failed to connect with this community." Rapidly growing churches are not content with a crowd. They want that crowd forged into a church. "I'm never satisfied with our process of assimilation," Jacob told us. "I'm constantly asking, 'How can we do this better?' Underneath the surface with the show, there's almost an obsession with doing assimilation better."

Scott Chrostek agrees that assimilation is everything. And Resurrection is simplified compared to many mainline churches. They also make it easy, user-friendly, fingertip-accessible to find out where to serve. And Chrostek sees the limits of preaching alone. At Resurrection the preaching is often pumped in via video. Other times the preacher is with the congregation live. "It wasn't the relationship folks were initially drawn to," Chrostek said. "It was the quality of the sermon. But that's not enough to bring about transformation of life." So one advantage of launching a campus where he didn't have to preach most of the time was that Scott *could* focus on building community, following up, devising systems to see that people not fall through the cracks: "That's as important as anything else in our story."

This is the largest untold story of megachurches writ large. The Methodist genius for small-group discipleship lives on in mega- and giga-churches that work hard to move people into discipleship relationships with Christ through other people. Ginghamsburg UMC and Saddleback aren't big because people like crowds. Who likes to fight for a parking place? They're not big because of the dazzling show. That's good enough to get someone to come once or twice, but not to commit. They're big because if you don't show up for church, someone will notice, and miss you, and call after you. If you're hurting, someone will pray with you; and when they are hurting, you will pray with them. Folks look around in one another's souls, ask where it hurts, and apply healing balm there. We do what early Methodists spoke of as "watch over one another in love." It's a radical act in our astonishingly impersonal age—to know another person by name and love them. And there is no church without this radical act.

If You're Not Accused of Being Superficial, You're Not Evangelizing Enough

Miofsky notes that folks often say of rapidly growing churches that they're sacrificing depth. He hears it so often, in fact, he passes on wisdom from Mike Slaughter in response: if you're *not* getting that complaint, you're not focusing on evangelism enough. If your focus is laser-like on reaching new people for the gospel, then you *will* have that complaint in your flank from long-time church types. If they're not whining about that, then you're coddling them too much. Recently Matt was asked to meet with a core group that had some questions. "We want to grow deeper," they said. "Okay," he responded. "How?" They answered: "We want to know the scriptures more intimately."

Matt paused. He could think of nowhere where Jesus said, "Okay, let's all dive into Isaiah." For Jesus, growing deeper meant *going out*, serving, carrying on his mission, exorcising demons, healing, preaching the kingdom. So Matt asked an awkward question back: "When was the last time one of you led someone new to Christ?"

Awkward silence. This is the sort of question we Methodists used to ask one another all the time.

"Let me challenge you then," Matt continued. "The scriptural way to grow is to turn inside out. Go out and serve. Challenge yourselves. Set out low-hanging fruit, a mid-level challenge, and something unbelievable. And then work at it. Encourage one another. You'll find that as you lead people more deeply into Jesus, you'll love him all over again."

And somewhere John Wesley smiled.

RAPIDLY GROWING CHURCHES LOVE THE LOCAL

Stop me if you've heard this one: A new pastor arrives in a new town to plant a church. He knows no one. But with a strong call from God and a willingness to knock on doors and wear himself out and pray, he builds a church from scratch. And now you, too, can parachute into a place cold, and if you pray and work enough, God will raise up a church around you.

The story is a lie. It does not happen. But it has a powerful grip over our imaginations. In the Protestant mainline especially, we notice someone with charisma and a story about a calling, and we would like to think it can work. It can. It just doesn't always, or even usually. And it certainly doesn't work like the paragraph above.

The churches we have studied for this book are not instant miracles. They were all planted long before they were planted. Not just years before, but decades before. All church is local, to riff off of Tip O'Neill's famous comment on politics. These churches show the wisdom in the statement for parish life. These churches are each a perfect fit for their town. This is not accidental. These pastors know their place. They love their towns. And their churches reflect that love. They wouldn't have sprouted the way they have without it.

We Started Years Before We Planted

One of the most surprising observations is that a large percentage of pastors from RGCs actually grew up in or very close to the places their churches now sit. Several of these pastors live and work where they grew up. They're not homebodies—they've gone off to other places for school, traveled, even lived and worked in other places. But they serve and pastor now in a place where little bits of their past sneak up behind them and kiss them on the cheek. For example, Jacob Armstrong says that while he may have planted Providence in Mt. Juliet eight or nine years ago, God actually began planting it twenty-five to thirty years ago. "You can't manufacture that with a planter dropped into a place they're not from," he said. Providence may have launched an unimaginable three months after plans were laid, but really the plans had been being laid for the better part of three decades. "It's no exaggeration to say that every week someone comes up to me with some connection. 'Oh yeah, my son played baseball with you!' or whatever. It's a huge advantage to be indigenous."

This may be surprising in that Mt. Juliet is one of the fastest-growing suburbs in America. Almost *no one* is *from* there. So Armstrong's localness is not only unusual; it's reassuring. *Someone* is from here, knows the history, can describe what building went in when. Suburbia is often an effort to mask history and particularity. But of course every place has some. Armstrong can lift it out and make gospel out of it. "In this fast-growing community, things have changed a lot, but folks are drawn to the familiarity of a guy from the community—it feels safe."

Armstrong gives an example of searching for space to meet in. This is Tennessee, where it seems every school building already has some church plant meeting in the cafeteria and the auditorium on the weekend. So he approached a school without such a Sunday obligation. With a tight window before launch, the church was desperate to find a venue. He went to meet with the principal, not mentioning that the location was "terrible" and it was the "last school available" in the area, and was giving the spiel about what Providence wanted to be. She suddenly interrupted him, blurting out, "I know who you are! My daughter went on her first date with your older brother!"

Jacob didn't know if this was his sign to leave: "Okay, thank you, ma'am, nice to meet you!" But instead the conversation deepened and the church had its building. (No word on how to be sure one's siblings treated their first dates with kindness. . . .) "It was positive. We felt our families had grown up in the same community, and she saw me as someone she'd want to help mentor. There were a lot of those things initially."

Love What They Love

Matt Miofsky also serves where he grew up. His grandparents worked in St. Louis. His parents live nearby. He attended college locally at Washington University. He even married his high school sweetheart, which would be adorable if he and Jess weren't so sickeningly in love. More than that, he loves St. Louis. He acts as a constant tour guide as we drive around town—"Oh look! There's Saint Louis University's new law school!" It's hard to talk about much else while with him in the Gateway City. He even apologizes for it at one point: "I'm sorry, I just love my town." St. Louis is not always spoken of with love. In 1904, it was America's fourth-largest city, hosting both the Olympics and the World's Fair. The NFL's Rams are not the only entity to leave since then. St. Louis has lost population every year since its zenith in the 1950s. Major corporations have dialed headquarters down to field offices; millions have packed up for better-paying jobs. If you have heard mention of St. Louis in the news in recent years, it might be for baseball's Cardinals; it might be for the killing of Michael Brown and protests in Ferguson. Unlike Armstrong's Mt. Juliet, there are not churches vying to plant in every school. In fact, even school buildings sit empty in many places.

Miofsky likes the underdog status. He roots for his town. Not because he sugarcoats the challenges the city faces—he's a realist. He just loves the spot, and he believes the church can be part of the turnaround that the city needs and is ardently working for. And that comes through in his way of talking about and to the place. "I want to know my city, to know its neighborhoods, to know how to speak to its people," he said. When I visit one of his sites, I meet The Gathering's tech guru and visual artist, a man named Stu. As Matt praises Stu's many and varied skills, Stu interrupts: "I'm the Jose Oquendo around here." For those not in the know, Oquendo was the Cardinals' utility infielder for a good decade in the 1980s. If you don't catch the local reference, neither Stu nor Miofsky is slowing down to explain it to you.

And this is the kind of indigenous knowledge that parachute church planters often lack. We have a demographer put a pin on a board for where a population will be growing (already a questionable tack). And we send a willing and charismatic young person there for three years with gradually declining funding, and they hit the coffee shops and try and meet people. This is the wrong way to do things. Miofsky grows impassioned enough his own words are worth quoting on this point: "Resurrection is actually fifteen years older than it

28

claims. Embrace is twenty years older than you would think from the website. When we parachute drop pastors into places and want them to start nine months later, and give them benchmarks from places like The Gathering or Impact, we're totally ignoring that. None of these places were overnight miracles. They just weren't." Miofsky advises seeing a person's track record for ministry in a community. What sort of impact have they had over the *years*, not months? Someone who's done well is "a great candidate to launch."

This is especially important in an age when younger people have such a strong sensitivity to inauthenticity. Their BS sensor is always on. If they sniff it, or someone doesn't know a place, their alarm goes off. Knowing a place allows you to speak in its accent, to know what remains unspoken, to touch a fear so deep no one will speak it aloud. And it covers over faults. When things aren't perfect or polished at first, folks will stick with you if your authenticity is high.

Embrace Church, the fastest of these fast-growers, was also planted years before it was planted by a local boy, though differently than the others. Embrace was actually conceived, we might say, a hundred miles north of Sioux Falls. There Cornerstone Methodist in Watertown, South Dakota, has long been a tall-steeple church in a county seat town—the sort of place in which Methodism used to thrive. The collapse of county seat towns has been bad for our denomination, and arguably bad for our culture generally—where now do folks get together, argue, hash out their differences, and learn to love someone with whom they profoundly disagree?[1] Cornerstone was also more evangelical than lots of churches in the UMC. Roger Spahr, its long-time pastor, describes how Methodists who wanted to plant churches a generation ago got frustrated and left conferences

---

1. I take this observation from a conversation with Bishop Scott Jones—that the coarseness of American politics and the decline of main street Methodism are not unrelated.

that were not interested. (Craig Groeschel of Lifechurch.tv is the most prominent example—one reckons the Oklahoma Conference would love to have his tens of thousands of worshipers.) In the Dakotas pastors more frequently stayed with the conference.

Cornerstone had a thriving youth group—one in which Adam Weber made a commitment to Christ. That youth group was a funnel to Sioux Falls—the region's fast-growing banking hub. And so every year Spahr had young parishioners leave Watertown, move to the Falls, and fall out of church altogether. So Spahr made a habit of traveling down to the Falls himself to meet with small groups of graduates from his church. And as he helped recruit Weber there to church plant as he graduated from Asbury, he could reassure him—there were already dozens of young people "on fire for Christ" in place. Cornerstone helped in other ways too—with support to the tune of $150,000 in the first four years, and all the concomitant support. The conference kicked in $250,000 more. (Note: it takes a healthy congregation to plant a church—not just a charismatic individual, not just a bankrolling conference.) Spahr is now a DS in that conference. Bishop Bruce Ough has also been an avid supporter of Embrace. So Embrace was planted long before it was planted. Not that this made for trouble-free existence—far from it. Weber is full of tales of authorities prior to Bishop Ough's tenure in the Dakotas Conferences trying to insist he use the name "Methodist" on the sign, that he fill out extra reports other pastors didn't have to, suspicious that his vision for planting was all surface and no depth. But the support alongside the critique mattered. And now it's the fastest-growing church we have in United Methodism.

Weber himself agrees that being local gives legitimacy and built-in networks. In one example, he asks in a sermon how many folks present have golden-edged Good News Bibles at home, figuring he'd have one or two hands go up. "Nearly everyone had one," he said. These were a common gift from Lutheran youth groups in the Dakotas, which like many mainline churches handed out Bibles to kids that would remain unopened. That little touch of familiarity says something: "He gets me, he knows me, I understand that." Embrace's boldest recent venture is to open a new campus (he almost says "key-ampus," his midwestern vowels are so long) in the Twin Cities. United Methodism is full of beautiful old buildings (and some newer ones, and some not-so-beautiful ones!) that churches have either withered in, or are barely hanging on in, not knowing how to renew themselves. Ough presented a comparatively newer building to Embrace, and they agreed to take it on, with preaching beamed in by video the way it is elsewhere in Sioux Falls. Not every local reference that's "normal" in the Dakotas will works in Minnesota: "There are just so many nitpicky little things I just take as normal, but they're not—they're just normal for Sioux Falls," he said.

All this celebration of the local and long-time pre-planting could drive a pastor to despair. How can she be in a place before she got there? It reminds me of a friend who was born in the Appalachian town where he grew up. But long-time locals insisted he wasn't from there. "How could I be *more* from here? I was *born* here!" Well, they explained, *your people* aren't from here. No word on whether *his* kids could "count" as locals.

Get There as Fast as You Can

Of course, not every pastor is from the place where he or she serves. As the clichéd bumper sticker slogan goes, they might not be from there, but they got there as fast as they could. Olu Brown is not from Atlanta. He speaks often of his upbringing and college education in Texas. The drawl in his vowels shows as much—he sounds more country than most Atlanteans. He came to Atlanta to study in seminary and stuck around as an associate pastor at Cascade, one of the city's grandest old United Methodist churches. While serving there he attended the weekly meetings of a building committee putting up a new structure. This wasn't in his area of responsibility, and there were a lot of other things he could have been doing on Saturday mornings. But years later he would find himself building an ambitious church in the same city. Impact was begun long before it was begun—in Olu's service elsewhere in the city.

Olu might not be from the ATL but his wife, Pharae Brown, most certainly is. "I grew up at Cascade. I know the place," she said matter-of-factly, and with gratitude. She also worked in executive positions at Coca-Cola and Home Depot, two little Atlanta-based niche start-ups. When she came to work for Impact Church, she had years of executive experience in some of Atlanta's most important business institutions. Her work for Impact was in graphic design— not even her professional specialty: "I didn't even major in marketing. I did finance," she said.

Impact, like Embrace, had support and encouragement from its parent congregation, Cascade. It also received people from its mother church, which can make for awkwardness for two churches in the same city, even if the sending church is amiable. "Half the people here are from Cascade," one parishioner tells me when I visit, perhaps exaggerating a little. Brown himself said he'd been building toward Impact's launch since his arrival in 1999: "Folks think I was appointed and started soon after, but actually I'd been working on Impact for years. I didn't just wake up one day and start from nothing."

Impact started with a can-do core group of twenty-five—folks from Cascade and elsewhere in the community who felt called by

God to do church in a different way in the city. When I visited, several parishioners said they experience Impact as a relief from more traditional churches—it's not nearly as "formal" or "rigid" as some of their previous church experiences. Dress is more casual than in some traditionalist churches—especially among African-American congregations. (Impact is not strictly an African-American church; it draws from multiple visible ethnic identities.) Twenty-five may seem like a lot—except that Craig Groeschel and Lifechurch start new campuses with … wait for it … seven hundred people. That's not a plant—it's a large church! Impact had no large church, just a small cadre of really committed people. And one of their strong commitments has been to giving back to the neighborhood.

Early in its life Impact was also looking for a meeting place, as Armstrong was in Tennessee. They approached a principal who was very reluctant. Once meeting together, Impact's launch team learned why. Other tenants of her building had been less than upstanding. There had been some vandalism, so she wasn't naturally trusting. Olu described it as an early victory for Impact that she said yes. "We became one of her best partners," Olu said, and Impact makes a point of emphasis giving back to its community. Members go out of their way to give gift cards to teachers, to volunteer at school, to make their corner of Atlanta a better place to live. This is part of being a local church, to being planted before they were planted, even though Brown isn't from there. Churches are called to be, as Andy Crouch puts it, "counter-cultures for the common good."[2] They show a different way of living than their neighbors, *in order to bless those same neighbors.*

---

2. The language comes from Andy Crouch in his book *Culture Making: Recovering Our Creative Calling* (Downers Grove, IL: InterVarsity, 2013).

Jorge Acevedo confesses he might be an outlier to our "rule" that churches plant long before they plant. He was a military kid, going to more schools than he could count on one hand, before settling in Orlando and planting roots there. Fort Myers is a very different sort of town. So different he didn't know where it was at first. "I thought I was going to Coral Gables," he said of the phone call he got from the bishop, which he thought was a ticket to Miami's high-rent district. "I thought I was going to be hanging out with Madonna!" Instead he was off to a blue-collar community. Grace Church is multisite, Jorge says, "but we're less like North Pointe [Andy Stanley's behemoth in Atlanta] and more like *Sanford and Sons*. Part of our mythology is we had to get up early Sunday and open up the doors of the bar we met in to let the smoke out and sweep out the beer bottles." Elegant it ain't.

But Jorge loves the place. It's his home now, not Orlando. He'll die there, he says. And this is a deeply spiritual commitment for him. Lots of alpha females and males have a plan for their career and execute it rigorously. Acevedo said that was making him crazy. So he let go. Told God to do whatever God wanted with his future. He'd be hands-off. And soon that call came. It wasn't where he would have chosen. But now he would never un-choose it. "I love this community. My eyes fill with tears whenever I fly back home. I have a passion for what God is doing here." And the grace born at Grace shows it. One local commitment can be seen in the sweeping out of those beer bottles. Acevedo started running Celebrate Recovery, a worship service for those in recovery, nearly two decades ago. Grace has some eight hundred people through its doors each week for one or the other recovery group. Whether cause or effect, Acevedo's preaching and Grace's worship are "forthright about our hurts and hang-ups." And while Grace is misidentified as "a recovery church," Acevedo says, some one-third of its people have come into the church through that route.

Laura Heikes isn't technically from Austin, though her hometown of San Antonio is also in the hill country of Texas. She did, however, originally train to be a missiologist. So she understands the importance of studying a local culture, getting to know it intimately, casting the gospel in terms that folks once foreign, now family, understand and embrace. She moved to Bee Creek with some trepidation. It had some promise as a recent church plant, but no guarantee of a future. Yet, she and her husband bought a house anyway. This was a sign they were invested in the community. They got a local cell phone number. They started sharing in the same thirty-five-minute commute to a grocery store that their neighbors in Bee Creek complain about with them. "I am most naturally and authentically myself here versus anywhere else I've lived," she said. And her love for the local paid off in her church's next big bet and bold move in mission. A community member who'd never given to the church asked her for a meeting. He asked whether Bee Creek had ever contemplated building a gym. No, she thought, but a bigger sanctuary would be nice. He asked her to think about it—there was no gym in the area for general use in that region. What if "we," he asked, built one to serve the community? He'd give the first million dollars. They prayed and said yes, and the church just recently opened a $2.5 million recreation facility, with a youth room, with no capital campaign and no debt. Her willingness to listen to local need made for a bold new venture in mission—one not in her original plan.

Chrostek's Detroit roots run so deep he has to wonder aloud why he would have chosen to live in another American League city. He describes attending a Royals game early in his time in Kansas City and noticing all the corporate names on top of the high-rises—and realizing he didn't know their names. But he did know all the names in Detroit.

But Chrostek already knew how to love a city that others have given up on. He calls his outsider status an "advantage" in successfully planting the Church of the Resurrection Downtown. He could see things with fresh eyes, notice things others couldn't. With a maniacal work ethic, Scott could also connect quickly. He soon knew the firms' names. He also knew to import help. His number two, Kelly Sisney, had lived downtown with her husband and they had grown up in the area. They were Chrostek's Sherpas in terms of getting to know the downtown urban core. "It's hard to go in without someone at the right hand who knows the story behind the community and its history," Sisney said. Soon Resurrection was worshipping in a bar next to a strip club and a tattoo parlor in a part of town that had no history of a church presence. Some years later Resurrection is building the first new mainline church cathedral in a downtown US city in recent memory.

What all these stories have in common are pastors who are absolutely in love with the places they live and the people they serve. They make it their mission to be invested in their communities, not just during work hours, but all the time. They live, work, play, preach, and invest locally. This has implications for all pastors, no matter if they grew up in the place they serve or not.

I (Matt) often have the opportunity to travel, speaking to pastors who want to start either a new ministry, a new church, or a second site of an existing church. Inevitably I will have a pastor raise their hand and ask me if they should live in the place where they are starting a new site or ministry. Recently a man explained to me that he lived thirty miles away. It was not possible for him to move to the new town, but he intended to spend a significant amount of time there. Moving wasn't really an option given some life circumstances and his spouse's job. He asked me what I thought (a setup if I have ever seen one!). I was careful with my answer—but challenging nonetheless. "If it were me, I would either move or start the site where I live." Long-distance pastoring doesn't work.

But the same choice is actually presented to all pastors, especially those in the United Methodist system. We are appointed to churches, and sometimes they are not in the places we would choose to live. When we move there, we have a choice to make. Either we can invest everything we have and are in that place, for as long as God has us there, or we can bide our time, doing our job, living in the house, but keeping the boxes packed in the basement. Our investment in a place makes a difference. I see it all the time, just in my own church.

Three of The Gathering's sites sit close to major universities in St. Louis, so we have a lot of students that are part of our church. Most of the students are quick to tell me that they are only "passing through" St. Louis. They are living here for a two-year graduate degree, or a three-year residency. They aren't staying. But I have noticed that given this reality, there are two ways a person can break. Some use this reality as a reason to never connect, to keep friendships at arm's length, and to resist growing roots. In short, they don't invest because they don't intend to stay. Others dive right in. They make friends, get involved, and invest in the place they live as long as they live there. You can guess which of these persons has a better experience during their time here. Investing matters.

I had a pastoral intern once who showed up to The Gathering and declared that he knew St. Louis was a baseball town, but he hated baseball. I told him that he ought to learn to love it then. He thought it would be inauthentic to pretend to love something that he didn't. I agreed. If you are pretending to love a place and its people, it will show. There is a difference between being inauthentic, or pretending to love something you don't, and doing everything you can to invest in a place, learning to love the people and understand what makes the place tick.

The same is true for pastors. We have to invest in the places where we are called to serve. We have to love those places, or spend our time and energy learning to do so. The difference it will make to our ministry is profound.

It wasn't easy. For all Resurrections's resources, it didn't send Chrostek with committed members or promised money that some plants boast. Resurrection Downtown started with nine core members—the Chrosteks and the Sisneys included. Attendance went from nine to four hundred in just five months. This great success yielded a great need for more space. So they took to worshipping in Grand Avenue Temple on Sunday nights—an (appropriately named) grand building with no air conditioning in a city that can swelter in the summer. One of their early leaders was a schoolteacher nicknamed "Mr. Van," fully named Bryan Van Osdale. One Monday morning back at work, Mr. Van was singing under his breath a song he'd learned in church. A fourth-grade student of his named Javon heard him singing, and asked about the song, and learned about the church. "What's it like?" Javon asked. "It's hot. Really hot," Mr. Van said. Javon took it upon himself to cut out a hand fan for Mr. Van. He encouraged others in his class to do the same. Three more classes joined in. And soon Mr. Van was delivering cut-out hand fans from a local elementary school to the "very hot" church in downtown Kansas City. They were covered with drawings, prayers, and well-wishes. "We received those fans at a time when we needed something," Scott said. "The heat did keep some people away. But we received a defining story. We used that one in our first capital campaign six months

38

later. It was pivotal, foundation, spurring us to extravagant generosity." And it made possible the funds for Resurrection Downtown's first building.

That story didn't happen because Scott was from Kansas City. It happened because God planted generosity in the heart of one child that spread to his teacher and to others. But it's a very Kansas City story—of one child from a difficult neighborhood doing something sacrificial, and beautiful, for a church to which he had no connection other than his teacher's soft song. And as Chrostek tells the story, it's clear his life is enriched for it, as is his church's and Kansas City's.

Christianity is a local story. We get this from our Jewish forebears. Abram is from one place—Ur of the Chaldees. He's told to get up and go to a new place, where he knows no one, nothing. And he goes. Through countless detours and wrong turns and U-turns God's people come to possess the land, and then explode out into all the world, in the diaspora and then in the church. We are commanded to love the local, because God does. God has one mom, one Jewish body, one people—the church. And yet we cannot control where we're born. We can respond to God's call, like Abram, to get up and go. *Then we have to love the place where we're sent.* Jacob Armstrong suggests a planter can come to love a new place, sure enough. They just need to know they're twenty-five years behind! But God has been raising up a people from the dust for thousands of years more than that. The moral of this chapter isn't to only plant in the place where you're born. It's to plant only in places you love.

RAPIDLY GROWING CHURCHES EXIST TO REACH THE NEXT PERSON

Rapidly growing churches are singularly, relentlessly, and unapologetically evangelical. They see everything they do through the lens of inviting people to follow Jesus.

In his *New York Times* bestselling book *Good to Great*, Jim Collins coined a term that has become pervasive in the business world—the *hedgehog concept*. The idea is simple and comes from a folktale about foxes and hedgehogs. Foxes know a lot of things; they are wily and cunning, coming up with a myriad of strategies to attack the hedgehog. The hedgehog, by comparison, knows one thing—curling up in a ball when attacked, with sharp spikes protruding everywhere. With all the ideas, strategies, and creative plans the fox comes up with, the hedgehog sticks to its one big thing and wins every time. The analogy to organizations is straightforward—while good organizations devise numerous ideas worth pursuing and strategies worth following, great organizations focus on one big thing and are relentless about pursuing it.

Enter churches. Most churches are passionate about many things. We want to invite new people, care for long-time members, tend to the sick, have a great adult discipleship ministry, develop compelling ministries for kids and teenagers, impact the world through advocacy and justice ministries, and serve the poor and marginalized in our midst. Most of these ministries are biblical and are to be expected. But the list often continues. A sports league for low-income youth, a quilters group, a volleyball league for singles, Wednesday night dinners for fellowship, a Saturday morning running group, and on and on. Pretty soon, good churches are stretched so thin doing one hundred good ministries that it is easy to see evangelism as just another ministry. By comparison, rapidly growing churches relentlessly, singularly, and unapologetically elevate the practice of evangelism and see every other ministry through this lens. They are a hedgehog, doing this one thing well day after day, week after week, year after year.

What the Church Is For

First, rapidly growing churches are singularly focused on evangelism. Let me explain. The term *evangelical* is a loaded term. "The word makes me twinge a little because it's so politicized," Jorge Acevedo said. Yet he's one of the most evangelical pastors in all of United Methodism. "We have to keep the fire tended around evangelistic outreach," he said, because otherwise, "the drift on outreach is always south." When we use the word in this book, we mean something like what Acevedo does. *Evangelical* is actually a simple word. It means inviting new people to follow Jesus. A quick survey of mission statements shows the singular focus of rapidly growing churches is on evangelism. The Gathering's mission statement reads, "To invite new people to become deeply committed followers of Christ." At Church of the Resurrection, all campuses share a purpose: "to build a Christian community where non-religious and nominally religious people are becoming deeply committed Christians." At Providence Church,

the vision is "to see those who feel disconnected from God and the church find hope, healing, and wholeness in Jesus Christ." Laura Heikes at Bee Creek says she'd be bummed if her church received one hundred new members by transfer from other churches. The number she watches is new professions of faith. "My heartbeat as a pastor is to tell people who don't know, or who had a bad explanation, just how wonderful it is to live life with God," she said.

In each example above, the focus is on one thing: connecting people to Jesus. This is evangelism! Every other ministry of the church is then seen as being in service to this one mission. Instead of "evangelism" being a separate committee alongside Christian education, worship, missions, and finance, evangelism is *the* lens through which each of these other ministries must see their work. The missions committee cannot just dole out money to nonprofits or organize workdays in the community. They now have to ask some new questions: How is our mission work engaging new people and helping them to know Christ? As we engage people in works of service and justice, how are we also facilitating a new relationship with Jesus, both among those "serving" and those "served"? The same is true of each of the other ministries. How is our kids' ministry engaging and inviting kids in our community who are disconnected? Are our worship services accessible to new people? Do our discipleship ministries teach new people what it means to follow Jesus (or is it just a means for "fellowship")? Every ministry area and every staff person, no matter what their role, should be asking themselves, "How am I engaging, inviting, and connecting new people to Jesus Christ?" This is the overriding question that rapidly growing churches are asking.

For example, Grace in southwest Florida recently opened a new dinner church in the poorest part of their community—the second-largest trailer park in North America. They launched in September

2016 with a goal of 80 people by Christmas. They had 160 by then as it turned out, with six baptisms. This site is only four miles from Grace's mother ship! But those folks would have never come to them. So Grace had to go to them, and did, and found twice the fruit they hoped in just four months. This sort of story seems miraculous to us now. It used to seem ordinary among us Methodists. What good is a revivalist sect if you're not reviving anybody? By contrast, Acevedo brings up the Nothing but Nets work of which United Methodism has been so very proud: "We break our arms patting ourselves on the back about mosquito nets, but that's not our business! We're in the disciple-making business." He has no qualm with saving lives from malaria. That's just not what we do best.

The Criticism You'll Get

To voice this singular focus on evangelism almost begs a push-back: What about other aspects of the gospel? Are they less important? Aren't you just concerned about numbers? It seems like you care more about people who aren't here yet than people who are? Isn't Jesus about more than just getting new people to do things? I (Matt) don't have to try hard to write these questions, because they are all questions I've been asked (in the last few days, in fact). In addition to being singularly focused, rapidly growing churches are also unapologetic about evangelism. Instead of skirting the issue, over-explaining it, seeing evangelism as just a growth strategy, or having misgivings about it, rapidly growing churches deeply believe in their mission to reach new people and preach and teach the message to their church.

Years ago, The Gathering was in a growth spurt, running out of room in our sanctuary, running four worship services, and barely keeping up with the new people coming. We were at a crossroads.

Should we settle in, deal with the people who are coming, and take the foot off the gas pedal with regards to invitation? Our answer was a resounding "no!" Our board determined that evangelism was not about growth; it was about being faithful to what we read in the Gospels. We decided to start a second site and invite our more mature Christ followers to leave a place that is comfortable to them and start a new site with the intention of sharing the good news of Jesus with new people.

To prepare, we read and studied as a congregation the story of Jesus sending out seventy (or seventy-two) of his followers. It was a natural progression in the Gospel of Luke. For the first ten chapters, new people were encountering Christ. His first followers witnessed him teaching, preaching, serving, and healing people who were often disconnected from God. Then in the tenth chapter, Jesus turns the table on his followers. He looks at them and essentially says, "Okay, now it's your turn. Just as you saw me do all of these things for the sake of disconnected people, now I want you to do it." It wasn't enough to be close to Jesus and to follow him. Jesus also wants his followers out there engaging new people in the world. Mature faith is not primarily pictured as memorizing scripture, growing close with a small group, being in worship each week, or serving on every church committee. Jesus nowhere responds to those who want more of God by saying, "Okay, let's all have a Bible study on Isaiah!" In the gospel, mature faith is pictured as taking up the work Christ did for us and offering it for others. That is, evangelism. At The Gathering, we teach this, preach this, and expect it from every area of our ministry. Far from apologizing for it, we believe that it is a sin *not* to do this. Evangelism is singular, a lens through which we see everything, and we pursue that focus unapologetically.

45

Don't Like Evangelism?
Fine. Do It Better.

Finally, rapidly growing churches are relentless in their pursuit of new people. They will try anything and everything, deploy the best of their people and resources, and shape every aspect of ministry to engage, invite, and connect new people to Jesus every single day. They are relentless in this pursuit—to the point of overriding other concerns. For example, Jacob Armstrong found himself wondering during a recent baptismal service if he should invite others to join in. In the Bible we see this—"Look, here is water, what is to keep me from being baptized?" the Ethiopian asks Philip in Acts 8. So Jacob made an invitation. Anyone who wanted to follow Jesus should start, that very moment. During the next song a woman approached Jacob. She wanted to be baptized. And Jacob noticed both he and she started to hedge. Well, maybe they could meet together and discuss it. There are some classes to take. We need to sort out theology. But Jacob couldn't get the Ethiopian eunuch story out of his mind. He finally said, "Why don't we do this right now?" She promised to run home and get a change of clothes. He figured that was it; she wouldn't be back. But she did come back right away. And he baptized her. Unplanned new life not from any programming of ours, but just from offering an invitation and not being too scared to make good on it. When Jacob told that story to his bishop, Bill McAllily, his eyes filled with tears. *This* is what we existed for at one time. It could be again.

This doesn't need to be a one-off story, a sort of rarity. Resurrection Downtown shows as much. They have PUSH cards available to the congregation every weekend. These invitation cards are for anybody to take and share with people they know. They set an expectation that every week people will want to take these cards and invite friends. At least once a quarter, they knock on the doors of their residential and commercial neighbors, meeting them, asking questions, and offering invitations. Far from being a start-up strategy, this practice of invitation has become an ongoing part of the rhythm of what it means for them to follow Christ, and they are relentless in pursuing it.

Neither of us owes our calling to ministry to a Methodist church. I (Jason) was baptized as a Methodist in Oklahoma and got dragged to Methodist churches in North Carolina a few times a year and hated it. I'd see how much longer each hymn had in it (inevitably seventeen verses, it seemed) and wonder how a man could drone on about such inanities for so many interminable minutes. My dad sent me to a Baptist camp, however, where counselors loved me, told me about Jesus, showed me the beauty of the scriptures, and prayed with me as I asked Jesus to be Lord of my life. I was "saved," as they say. But I quickly soured on the Baptist churches I got to know. Their gospel seemed bound up with partisan politics. (I'll let you guess which party.) They'd get defensive when criticized. Only boys got to preach. So I wound up in an evangelical church that had none of those things. And finally in college the good preaching was going on in...wait for it...a Methodist church. They preached an intellectually satisfying gospel that didn't stop with the head but reached also for the heart. I was sunk. Still am. I love Methodism—we're a revivalist branch of the Catholic tradition that's passionate about social justice.

So why didn't anyone tell me at that boring church I got dragged to when I was growing up? Would it have killed them to say the J-word once in a while?

Here's the thing I learned after I went to seminary, got ordained, and started preaching: that boring old Methodist church had done me some good. I heard its preacher in my head as I started preaching. In other words, some of my criticism of it was misplaced. In my evangelical fervor I was mad at a mainline church for being so liberal as to leave out Jesus. But they didn't. They just didn't forefront evangelism. They didn't talk about reaching new people with the gospel. To do so would have seemed unseemly; it would have evoked fears of Elmer Gantry-like hucksterism, reminded them too much of "those" churches—backwoods ones that hate gay people and black people and non-Republican people.

The Romans used to say that the abuse of a thing doesn't negate its right use. (*Abusus non tollit usus.*) If someone murders someone with a hammer, don't ban hammers. Arrest the murderer. And use hammers to hammer nails, not to hammer people. The right response to evangelism done badly is evangelism done well. And we have a gospel worth evangelizing about. Here's the thing—without those Baptists I'd have never known Jesus. He's the organizing center of my life and heart, and the good news I'm trying to spend my life sharing with the world. And we Methodists keep him bottled up, mention him only by indirection, leave the cookies on the high shelf, worry more about offending our fellow NPR-listening neighbors than the people God craves who are dying to hear there's more to being human than your bank account or who you sleep with?!

Methodism started as a revivalist sect within the Anglican church. If our Anglican forebears had agreed to return evangelism to pride of place in church life, there'd have been no Methodism. But they didn't. All that warmhearted enthusiasm, the crying and the weeping and the preaching to poor people and organizing your life around prayer and fasting and service—it all seemed too . . .

uncivilized. Methodism took off in the Americas: a gospel that our whole life can be full of the radiance of God, that Jesus's kingdom is indeed coming, that all creation will be blessed—that is a beautiful gospel. It still is. Churches that talk about it even a little find people turning up to listen. Churches that talk about it a lot, well, they're like the ones we profile here.

Evangelism Won't Fix Decline

Too often, churches see evangelism as a means to some other end. When finances are tight, Sunday school numbers are dwindling, or the sanctuary is looking empty, we up the evangelism talk. Evangelism becomes an antidote to decline, a way for the church to steady itself and get back to a place of stability. To the extent that this ever works, and churches are able to gain a sense of stability, often the evangelism stops. We want enough new people to keep the church stable, enough growth to make up for the natural decline, but we don't make the pursuit of new people a core activity, an essential part of what it means to follow Jesus. In fact, many churches want to strike a balance. They may not say it, but they sure act like it. We want enough new people so that the church's future seems secure but not so many new people that they cause us to change what we love about our church. We certainly don't want new people to take over leadership or change the culture of our congregation. We want new people who basically like what we are already doing and want to become a part of it, but not so many that they disrupt the nice, meaningful, and pleasant experience that we have spent generations cultivating. This is the unspoken mind-set of many congregations.

Not so long ago, the board of a neighboring church asked me (Matt) to come speak with them about how to attract new people.

They asked me to meet them in the parlor, where they held their board meetings. When I arrived, the room looked like my grandmother's living room, complete with pink walls and carpeting, a china cabinet, and a sofa that looked like something off *Antiques Roadshow*. I walked in and immediately asked about the room: what is it used for, who meets in it, and so forth. They shared with me that they host a variety of events from meetings to membership classes to welcoming new people. I asked them how important the room was and if they were willing to change it in order to make it more compelling for new generations of people. The answer was a resounding "No." Like too many churches, they wanted me to teach them how to attract new and younger people without changing too many things that are highly valued, from paint colors to furniture to worship.

Ken Carter is a fabulous Methodist bishop in Florida. He inherited a conference whose downward trajectory was even sharper than the rest of Methodism. Why? Because, he says, Methodism's growth strategy in Florida for decades was simple: wait for Methodists in the Midwest to retire, move to Florida, and join the nearest Methodist church. And that worked for a while. The problem is the Midwest is plumb out of Methodists. And when people move to a new place, they don't search for church by brand. They search for a church that talks about God in ways that move them to love God and neighbor. If they search for a church at all—increasingly in retirement meccas new people take offense when asked if they want a suggestion for a church. "We've never been to church," they'll say, and if pressed will rehash cultural accretions about our being intolerant, homophobic, bigoted, corrupt. We have to fight to get people now. Other industries know this—restaurants, coffee shops, universities, vacation spots—these don't sit back and wait for people to find them. They go after people. Surely the gospel is infinitely more valuable. Can I get an amen, Methodists?

Rapidly growing churches approach evangelism differently. It isn't a side activity deployed as a means to counteracting natural decline. Instead, it is relentlessly pursued as a value every day in every aspect of the ministry. Evangelism is a lens through which everything in the church is viewed. It does so because God longs to be in relationship with everyone. At The Gathering, if we are picking out paint colors for the lobby, deciding on a title for a new sermon series, finalizing a financial budget, or debating a worship element, the first question we ask is always, "How does this help us invite new people to follow Jesus?" The answer guides our work every single time. One pastor explained it this way: Churches naturally drift toward what they like and what has worked for them in the past. Like throwing a leaf in a river, the natural movement is downstream. Thinking of new people takes constant and relentless effort—it is like walking upstream. In other words, we don't have to work to think of the needs of the people who are already here. But if you want to prioritize new people, you have to put effort into it every single day, no matter how small or large the decisions. Rapidly growing churches are relentless in evangelism—they wake up and prioritize it every day.

Because God Loves Your Neighbor

Methodism was born as a revivalist sect. The question is—if we're not reviving anybody, what do we exist for? The answer is we won't for long. And we shouldn't. Why bother if God isn't renewing the cosmos—and inviting us to join in? And this may be the most exciting opportunity for evangelism of all: why we do it. There have been times when evangelicalism has exerted its zeal to save people from hell. If we don't evangelize, people go to the place with the pointy sticks. It's safe to say salvation from hell does not figure large on our list for evangelizing anymore. And, arguably, it shouldn't. Hell doesn't come up often in the scriptures, and it's brought out some of our worst and most manipulative moments as Christians, trying to strike fear into people so they'll do what we want. Instead of that, we get to evangelize for a positive reason: for Jesus, the life he invites all people to. Jesus is the sort of good news you can't keep unless you give it away. And Jesus has decided, despite all the good reasons not to, to marry his bride, the church. If you want him, you have to go through her, and vice versa. And if you want him, he's there. And he's bringing all the other people he loves with him—including our enemies, the poor, social outcasts, even...evangelicals. And by the time you're done with him, you'll be all those things too.

RAPIDLY GROWING CHURCHES ELEVATE THE PRACTICE OF GIVING

Rapidly growing churches elevate the practice of giving, teach proportional giving, and effectively talk about and manage money.

What churches believe about generosity matters greatly, but how they live out that belief perhaps matters more. Most churches are caught in a contradiction. They believe that generosity is an essential component of faithful discipleship and that Jesus challenged his followers to use their resources for the sake of the kingdom. Most pastors and churches believe this. Yet in practice, most churches do not build cultures of generosity, teach the importance of giving, or talk about money with the frequency and fervor that Jesus did. In many cases, churches have adopted practices that actually contradict their beliefs about money.

Have you ever been to a church that actually tells new people *not* to give? The result is a mixed bag of inconsistent and contradicting messages about money, generosity, and the importance of giving as part of following Jesus and growing in faith. In the midst of this confusion, rapidly growing churches elevate the practice of giving, teach tithing (or proportional giving), and effectively talk about and manage money.

Unlearning Bad Behavior

Before churches can learn new behaviors around giving, they usually have to unlearn bad behavior that has been picked up over the years from past churches, old "best practices," and misguided notions of what it means to welcome guests. We all pick up some of these habits along the way. For those who have grown up in the church, especially the mainline church, we have several such habits to unlearn.

1. *Churches don't talk about money.*

Some churches simply stay silent on money. The rationale changes from place to place. Sometimes leaders are afraid that money conversations will anger people in the pews. Others fear that new people will be turned away. Some notice the bad reputation that the church "only talks about money," so they choose to never talk about money. Perhaps there are pastors who themselves are uncomfortable with the topic and therefore do not naturally weave it into their teaching and preaching. Whatever the reason, the result is the same: churches are silent on one of the most important components of discipleship. This hurts not only the people who are seeking to grow in faith, but also the church's ministry that depends on the faithful practice of generosity.

2. *Churches talk about money when they are desperate.*

This is usually the result of the first mistake. We never talk about money until we absolutely have to, and by that time, there are usually problems. How many of you have heard this kind of announcement? It is late November. The finance team realizes that the church won't make budget. Certain big givers have died or are not coming through as in previous years. Expenses have crept up. Reserves are depleted. So they reluctantly decide that they have to go to the congregation and help them understand how dire the situation is. Someone from the committee gets up on Sunday morning, usually with charts, graphs, spreadsheets, and slides, and explains the situation. Then, there is the plea: "Please give so that we can meet budget, keep up our ministry, and maintain the building." Ironically, we believe that if we wait until things are desperate enough, this will not only motivate people to give but help them understand why we had to bring it up. Sometimes this works—the budget is met, and money talk goes into hibernation until the whole cycle repeats itself. Increasingly, though, this strategy doesn't work. Part of this is common sense. People do not give out of loyalty the way they once did. People are not motivated to bail out a struggling institution. People want to give to something that is exciting, making an impact, and visibly connected to changing lives. To talk about giving only when times are tough might make a certain kind of "sense" to church leaders of a generation ago, but it is disconnected from the realities of why people give now.

3. *Churches only talk about money in connection to giving.*

This is another critical error. There are many churches that avoid talking about money except when they need to talk about giving. What happens is Pavlovian in effect. Every time the congregation hears "money," they assume you are about to ask them to give it to you. The effect is that they arm themselves with justifications and excuses, or avoid you altogether. On the practical level, many churches commit this error when they preach and teach about money once a year during stewardship season. Over time, not only do we associate money talk with giving talk, but we fail to teach the breadth of what scripture challenges people to do with their resources.

A corollary to this mistake is that we associate generosity with giving to the church, because every time we talk about the practice of generosity, we are asking people to be generous toward "us." Together these errors compound the belief in people that the church "always talks about money" or "only wants my money." In fact, the church ought to be a community that helps people think faithfully about their finances.

4. *We ask new people not to give.*

In many ways, trying to correct previous mistakes creates new ones. In fact, this mistake is most often made by newer churches, contemporary churches, or churches trying to connect with new people. Here is the reasoning: One of the stereotypes new people have about the church is that they are only after money. One of the reasons people stop giving to church is the belief that the church was always after their money. The corrective seems obvious—we will actually ask them not to give!

I was visiting a church recently, and when the offering time came around, the pastor stepped up and shared something like this: "Here at our church, we give as a part of worship, but if you are new or have just recently started coming, we do not expect you to give. Your presence is gift enough." Now on the surface this seems reasonable. After all, we want new people to feel welcomed, we do not want the offering to be a moment of pressure or awkwardness, and we do not want to send a wrong message that we value people less for who they are and more for what they can give us. But the result of this reasoning is

56

ironic. We actually teach new people not to do the very thing that we later invite them to do. To think about this differently, substitute giving with a different Christian practice. What if, for example, before the opening prayer we said, "Now at our church we pray, but if you are new, we do not expect you to pray with us. Just sit there and listen to us do it"? Or what if we said, "Here at our church we listen to the scripture read and preached, but we don't expect that from new people. So if you'd like, go ahead and step out, and we will invite you back in when we are done"? These are somewhat silly examples, but you get the point. Most people do not need to be given permission not to give. They protect their money quite well. The invitation not to give only makes it more difficult later on to introduce the practice of generosity.

5. *We talk about giving apologetically.*

Even if many churches do not outright ask people not to give, many speak about giving apologetically. We over-explain, offer conditions, and sometimes outright apologize before we ask people to practice generosity. We focus on how hard it is and how tired we know many people are of hearing about giving. We remind them that they do not have to give, and talk about giving in sacrificial terms. But generosity helps us grow closer to Christ and leads to greater joy in our lives.

These are just a few of the habits and assumptions churches have picked up over the years. In the midst of a church culture that sends mixed messages around money and generosity, rapidly growing churches unapologetically elevate the practice of giving, teach proportional giving, and effectively talk about money.

Scott Chrostek, pastor of Church of the Resurrection Downtown in Kansas City, talks about the way that giving was woven into the preaching from the very beginning. Resurrection Downtown taught tithing in the first year with a largely millennial congregation that was new to church or nominally connected. That set the stage for them to do a capital campaign just fourteen months into their launch. Through the campaign, even they were surprised at how receptive people were to the message of generosity. The giving was so extravagant that from that point on, they decided not to focus on tithing because it actually *limited* what new and existing people may otherwise give! This small example illustrates a few patterns that we discovered in rapidly growing churches.

What to Do Instead

1. *Talk about giving often and early.*

With the rise of seeker-sensitive worship, giving was left in a precarious position. Popular wisdom holds that people are turned off by institutions asking for money. Giving and asking for money contribute to why people don't go to church, right? The answer, it turns out, is no. In *UnChurched*, Gabe Lyons and David Kinnaman talk about why young people have stopped attending church.[1] Talking about money is not included. A cursory scan of the literature will show that this reason is more in the imaginations of church people than in the hearts of unchurched people.

Rapidly growing churches understand that new generations of people want to make a difference in the world and are looking for compelling ways that they can be a part of impacting the lives of others. Therefore, growing churches talk about giving early and often, showing how generosity helps to change the lives of others.

---

1. Gabe Lyons and David Kinnaman, *UnChurched: What a New Generation Really Thinks About Christianity . . . and Why It Matters* (Grand Rapids: Baker, 2012).

At The Gathering, the offering plays a prominent role at Christmas and Easter—the peak times for new guests. Through the practice of donating 100 percent of these monies away, we use the offering to promote missions, talk about the way the church is impacting the world, and proudly invite people to be a part of it. Giving is extraordinary during these times. In 2015, the Christmas Eve offering alone surpassed $250,000, much of that given by guests and first-time attendees.

Rather than asking new people not to give, thereby creating a bad habit that has to be undone later, growing churches link giving to mission and invite people to participate from the beginning.

2. *Ask people to give when times are good.*

It seems counterintuitive. Why talk about it when everything is going well? The idea is simple. Because when things are going well, people are eager to lend their support. And when people are excited to support ministry, they are much more willing to give. No one wants to support a sinking ship. But everyone wants to get on board with something that is making a difference. Rapidly growing churches use success stories to talk about giving, because they understand that giving is a way for people to participate in the amazing work that God is doing.

Adam Weber, pastor of Embrace Church, has a habit of meeting with eighty families in his church each year to talk about giving. He doesn't need their money to keep the lights on. Rather, he uses this opportunity to talk about the amazing work God is doing through Embrace and his vision for doing even more. Last year alone this meeting produced an additional $250,000 for missions. Talking about giving when people can see the fruit of the work all around them only excites them to give even more. Rapidly growing churches use successes and ministry celebrations as an opportunity to talk about giving.

3. *Teach new people about the benefits of generosity and the joy of giving.*

> The one who supplies seed for planting and bread for eating will supply and multiply your seed and will increase your crop, which is righteousness. You will be made rich in every way so that you can be generous in every way. Such generosity produces thanksgiving to God through us. Your ministry of this service to God's people isn't only fully meeting their needs but it is also multiplying in many expressions of thanksgiving to God. They will give honor to God for your obedience to your confession of Christ's gospel. They will do this because this service provides evidence of your obedience, and because of your generosity in sharing with them and with everyone. They will also pray for you, and they will care deeply for you because of the outstanding grace that God has given to you. (2 Cor 9:10-14)

Rapidly growing churches teach people about the benefits of generosity and the joy of giving. If we truly believe that Jesus taught his followers to be generous, and if we really believe that giving helps us grow closer to Christ, then we would connect the dots for people to see the joy of giving. We would never ask someone *not* to do something that we believe makes them happier, healthier, and better able to follow Jesus.

While the idea of sacrifice plays a role in a theology of giving, rapidly growing churches tend not to talk about giving as a sacrifice. They rather talk about giving as a gateway to joy and contentment.

In 2013, *The Wall Street Journal* published an article on the science behind giving. Among other things, scientists found that our brains are actually hard-wired to experience satisfaction when we give.[2] When people give, the same part of the brain that regulates

---

2. See here Elizabeth Svoboda, "Hard-Wired for Giving," *Wall Street Journal* (Aug 31, 2013): https://www.wsj.com/articles/hardwired-for-giving-1377902081?tesla=y.

pleasure related to food and sex lights up! Through the release and reception of serotonin and oxytocin, generosity unleashes a neuroscience chain reaction that leads to satisfaction, pleasure, and social binding. All this points to a deeper truth—God hard-wired us to give, and when we operate in a manner that is consistent with our creation, good things happen in our life. Giving is not only about sacrifice, but it is (perhaps more) about living as we were created to live, with joy and satisfaction.

When we lead conversations about money with metaphors of sacrifice, we condition people to see giving as a duty to be suffered. But rapidly growing churches also talk about the joy and satisfaction people experience from giving, thereby rewriting the narrative around generosity. At The Gathering, we made a decision early on that when we talked about giving we would consistently connect it with good outcomes: lives impacted, testimonies of change in the lives of the givers, and the difference made beyond the walls of our church. Giving is no longer an obligation to suffer through but a blessing to experience.

One Sunday at Impact Church in Atlanta, the pastor inviting us to give an offering told a story. She and her husband were in line for brunch when a homeless person approached them, panhandling. They gave a dollar, perhaps thinking of their child watching nearby and trying to live out the generosity to which the church calls us. Their child had a few further questions, though. "Mom, didn't you just say you got out one hundred to give to your friend at a wedding tonight?" Yes. "Doesn't this woman need it more?" Yes. "Isn't she Jesus, like they say at church?" Soon the Benjamin came out and was in the homeless woman's hand.

The family watched what happened next with astonishment. The panhandler proceeded back down the line of those waiting for brunch, *giving back the money she'd received.* She rejoiced. She celebrated. And she gave people back the money she'd gotten from them. Generosity begets generosity. And do you see what Jesus meant when he constantly told us the poor are blessed? This one poor woman experienced the joy of giving just as they had when they gave to her before (warning: what goes around doesn't always come around *this* fast!).

Notice what this story teaches the church: that giving is good, it humanizes us, it multiplies joy, it shows how delightful it is to be part of humanity. And you don't even have to be rich to do it. Is there any wonder it makes for some of Jesus's best parables?

4. Celebrate what giving accomplishes in actual people's lives.

For too long, churches have connected giving with "keeping the lights on," "meeting budget," or "continuing the work of the church." Rapidly growing churches connect giving to concrete change in the lives of people.

At The Gathering, testimonies (both live and via video) are a big part of weekend worship. Whether part of the sermon, the offering, or elsewhere in worship, we share stories of what God is doing in the lives of people. During the offering, we make an extra effort to connect giving to the stories that people just heard. When we ask people to give, we often say something like, "Your giving makes stories like the one we just heard possible. Your gift will not only change you, but it impacts the lives of the people around you in more ways than you realize." This is a simple move, but the accumulation of this practice is staggering. Over time, people come to associate giving with concrete changes in the lives of people. And guess what? People love to give to things that are making a visible difference.

Laura Heikes says that elevating the practices of generosity is one of the things that Bee Creek Methodist has done with the most intentionality. During her first year, a lay leader spoke up at a finance meeting. The rest of the group was proud that making budget was within reach. But this leader said she was troubled that a church that claims to believe in missions was only giving away one percent of its budget. As ever, budgets are moral documents, and this one showed the church cared less about its neighbors than it thought it did. The church worked to move that number to ten percent within five years. They arrived in three. Every week Heikes includes a story somewhere in worship of what folks' giving accomplishes. "Stewardship Sunday" is no more, replaced by "I love my church Sunday," with testimonies from ten people (!) on how the church has changed their lives. And in teaching about membership, folks are told they are expected to give three hours a week—one in worship, one in service, and one in prayer—*and* to move toward the biblical tithe of ten percent. Far from apologizing for talking about money, Bee Creek shows what Jesus taught—that to get to our hearts God must go through our wallets.

5. *Talk about money and not just giving.*

One of the unintended consequences of never talking about money except when we need it, is that when a congregation hears the topic "money," they automatically associate it with "giving." Churches often overlook the reality that even if people wanted to give, they often first have to undo years of poor financial management just to begin this new practice. Jesus talked holistically about money, possessions, and our relationship with what we have. Giving was a critical part of a larger whole.

63

Rapidly growing churches talk holistically about money throughout the year in order to help people live more faithfully in relationship to their finances. Adam Weber at Embrace Church talks about the way his church shifted the timing of the traditional "stewardship" season. While most churches do this in the fall, Embrace decided to do it in January, right after the holidays. The reasoning was that in the wake of Christmas, people have to deal with poor financial choices and the aftermath of overspending. While it may not seem like the best time to ask people for money, it is a great time to teach people about the faithful management of money. Through teaching people more biblical money management habits, churches can set the stage for generosity.

For example, Grace Church in southwest Florida noticed how ineffective it was to talk about money only with anxiety or guilt when the church budget gets tight. So instead of haranguing, they offered a series of sermons and courses called "Free," and promised how good it would feel to get from "here to there," as Pastor Jorge Acevedo said. The problem is most of us haven't been taught about money at all, but we have been taught to be voracious consumers, so many of us are in debt—the opposite of freedom. Grace offered a version of Financial Peace University, led by a pastor. Two hundred families went through the course, and retired more than $700,000 worth of consumer debt *in nine weeks*. The church's giving went up accordingly without a word about tithing or giving to the church. Here the church modeled what it means to live a flourishing life— free of rapacious credit card companies—and free to give more of us to God and neighbor.

At The Gathering, we preach about money throughout the year. We often will dedicate an entire series to money and faith *without* asking people to give money. This helps build credibility with a congregation by showing that we care about their financial health and not just getting their money. When we later preach about generosity and giving, people have already started financial habits that make a response possible.

RAPIDLY GROWING CHURCHES WORK IN TEAMS

One of our hypotheses is that fast-growing churches have talented number twos in place. Their senior minister is no solo genius. In fact, anybody "in the know" knows that behind the scenes is an administrator, or associate pastor, or executive pastor, or whatever they're called, without whom the church would not be anything like what it is. The number two doesn't dive for the microphone. He or she has no designs on the senior pastor's job. They are there to offer the highest level of competence in support of the church's mission. They're a sounding board and trusted source of advice for the pastor. They're often dear personally to their senior. Scratch hard at any success story among church planters and you'll find such a number two. Or several.

As we researched some of the fastest-growing Methodist church plants in America, we found this hypothesis confirmed in each case. The number two is a person who has sacrificed personally for the sake of the congregation's mission. They have become loyal to the vision of the congregation more than to the pastor personally. They have brought expertise from other kinds of work experience outside the church. And their gifts have complemented the very different gifts of the pastor and church planter. In each case, that person says he wouldn't be where he is without the number two. The number two could be doing any number of other jobs with a high degree of excellence.

In other words, an excellent leader is necessary for a rapidly growing church, but not sufficient. Without the number two, the best number one in the world isn't going to get you far.

The Solo Genius Doesn't Exist

Think of the number twos in popular imagination. There is no Frodo Baggins without Samwise Gamgee. There is no Tina Fey without Amy Poehler. There is no Don Quixote without Sancho Panza. There is no Sherlock Holmes without Dr. Watson. Perhaps the great number two in pop culture is one Commander Spock. He is the ideal yin to Captain Kirk's yang. Kirk is impulsive, domineering, aggressive. Spock is cool, analytical, *logical*, to invoke his favorite word. Kirk is the warrior captain of *Star Trek's* great starship, the *Enterprise*. Spock is its science officer who can suss out the mystery behind any conundrum linguistic, biological, or extraterrestrial. Spock could have his own ship (and occasionally he does). He can handle himself in a fight. But his purpose in the universe is to keep Kirk, and the *Enterprise*, and their mission, alive and flourishing. His human companions tease him. "You green-blooded inhuman!" Bones shouts at him at one point. He responds with merely a half-raised eyebrow. Spock is the clear number two. There is no question of usurping Kirk's place in the captain's chair. But if Spock weren't sitting behind it, that chair would be empty. Or obliterated.

The illustration is silly, of course. But then the number two often brings a silliness that number ones cannot afford. Kelly Sisney is

Scott Chrostek's number two at Church of the Resurrection Downtown in Kansas City. She tells of a phone call she received when Resurrection started downtown from a man asking if they welcome people who follow "alternative lifestyles." She paused. "What are you, a pirate?" she asked. He laughed, turned up on Sunday, and stuck around—their first member. Her skills as a former stand-up comedian came in handy. Scott Chrostek is a funny man. Successful pastors often are. But he has nothing on his number two. She wasn't just successful in defusing a phone call that could have been awkward, or even a PR disaster; she diffuses radiance. Number twos have to be good gatekeepers for the number one—knowing when to involve him or her, and especially when not to. Here Sisney did more than book an appointment for the senior. She took away the need for one. She passed on the heart of the church. Resurrection Downtown doesn't have special "in" people and "out" people. Or if there are, Jesus takes the side of the "out," and so does the church. Number twos believe in and embody the missional heart of their congregation, and go around diffusing that heart's radiance in whatever they do. For it's the heart of Jesus.

We see here the threefold gifts that a number two needs for her or his crucial mission. They have to be loyal in three ways: First to God, and to a mission bigger than him- or herself. This is crucial for a church to be high-functioning. Successful organizations are often filled with yes people at the top. The number two has to be willing to tell the person in charge when they're dead wrong. Secondly, the number two has to be loyal to the congregation's mission. Folks will immediately ask about churches with only one employee, who obviously cannot employ a number two for anything. These folks often joined in the church's mission when they were also small. Long before they were paid, they intuited what Sunday school teacher needed encouragement, what parent needed help, what problem they could solve before the pastor even noticed it. Even if the church never grows past hiring one employee, it needs leaders like that—and has them, if we are paying attention. Three, the person needs to be loyal to the senior him- or herself. There has to be a special chemistry between these two. Before Laura Heikes of Bee Creek UMC makes a key decision, she says she has to check "with the other half of my brain"—in her case, key lay leaders and staff who are good at managing details. Laura knows that visionary leadership needs nuts-and-bolts know-how and looks to staff and laity gifted in these areas. The pastor can't be wondering whether she can trust that right-hand person. We might think of these three loyalties as making up a three-legged stool—each is equally important—and without any one of the three, things come unglued.

Jorge Acevedo, senior pastor of Grace Church in Cape Coral, Florida, speaks of his conversion often. He had a first conversion, in terms of both timeline and importance, to Christ, in 1978. He had a subsequent conversion to the importance of the church as the bride of Christ in 1992. His third conversion, dated to 2006, was to turn from being a heroic leader to a "generative team leader." Before that, if he'd been hit by a bus, Grace's ministry was done. He hadn't done enough to raise up other leaders, to push the work out, to make himself inessential. Now he has. He only preaches some eighteen to nineteen Sundays a year. "I've gotten my personal life back," he says, preparing him to serve in other ways and sustainably for a longer working life. He reduced his direct reports from forty to four. And all of this was possible partly because of his number two, who came through his youth group and has been a friend for a third of a century. The literature on church growth doesn't normally emphasize this, but we can't say it strongly enough—number twos are lifesavers not just for the number one, but for the whole church.

Dan Lins started at Providence by plugging in cords for guitar amps before the sun came up on Sunday morning. He was a successful attorney in Nashville, loving the energy of a thriving law firm. He was doing things for businesses that most of the rest of us can't understand, with the firm's head becoming a player in city politics. He'd gone into the law at least partly to make good money, and he was doing that. But he'd also found the church, and a gospel he'd been looking for, and that calling to something outside of ourselves, bigger than ourselves, worth giving ourselves over to. He didn't just join; he volunteered. (On behalf of all pastors everywhere, let me stop and say: thank you!) He thought he might get to do something important. They asked him to turn up for church at 5:30 a.m. and plug in cords for the praise team. To be a roadie. On a day when most professionals with any sense get up late and wear pajamas all day. The morning pregame before church is intense—especially if you're in borrowed space and the whole thing has to be set up before sunrise and taken down after reasonable people have gone to lunch. Dan dove into the least glamorous part of that.

A successful restaurant chain in Canada has as its philosophy that anyone in the organization has to do the lowest jobs first. You can't be a server unless you've bussed. You can't be a cook unless you've washed dishes. You can't be a manager unless you've done all of it. The church should have come up with this first. In fact, we may have; we just don't crow about it. What pastor hasn't been called to triage an emergency with a plunger? For example, Matt points out that Sabra Engelbrecht at The Gathering in St. Louis started her work at the church volunteering in the church kids' ministry, and offering her services through the church as a lawyer to vulnerable people in

71

town. She has the capacity to do any job in the building—and was happy to start with the "lowest." Lord, send us more like that.

Any pastor worth their salt notices talent. These folks have it. For example, Lins served on committees at Providence. He became a lay leader—in Methodism this is the key position that gives someone the inestimable privilege of serving on every committee there is. (God spare us all.) He likes putting together budgets, working with spreadsheets, mastering details—the very things most pastors are sorry at. The church had grown to seven hundred with Jacob Armstrong as the only full-time paid staff person—a growth that has not abated still. As it ran a search for an executive pastor position, Lins felt compelled to apply. And only then did he decide to tell his spouse! It would mean an $80,000 pay cut.

One day at work he looked out over the city's beautiful Centennial Park. He says he felt an overwhelming sense of peace. If God wanted him to do this, God would provide for his family. They would lack for nothing. God's voice wasn't quite audible, but it was there, bringing a reassurance that "flooded" his heart. He applied. Folks at the church said he was the toughest, meanest guy there. Funny—because at the law firm he was chided for being the most gentle! Apparently our churches need some toughness; he got the job and hasn't looked back. The Linses have adjusted to living on less; his wife calculated all their expenses for the year to announce they had a little left over—$1.20 left over, to be precise. God provided just enough—with a vending machine Coke to spare.

Don't You Dare

Sisney agrees that growing churches need a number two with backbone. She describes being in meetings where folks are criticizing

Resurrection Downtown: "And they're all sitting around using pastory words with their pastory faces, and I want to say, 'Don't you dare say that to my church!'" Travis Waltner at Embrace in South Dakota jokes that he worked in a juvenile detention center before he ever worked at the church—so he wouldn't be intimidated in a committee meeting. Olu Brown speaks of needing someone who is both a challenge and a partner, and so he names things he's not good at that he hopes a number two will be: "detail-oriented, people connected, with great coaching ability, and *not conflict averse*." With backbone to spare.

It strikes us that the call stories of number twos are as important, as dramatic, as life-changing as those of the pastors they serve. This is no accident: Methodists are people of the revival tent and the warm heart that John Wesley spoke of and inspired in others. Vibrant experience of the Holy Spirit's challenging presence runs deep in our heritage. It just feels sort of hackneyed now, like Sunday school felt figures and ladies' big hats. Cute, but we don't really do it. Except these folks do. Is it any accident they're of such service to their churches?

A meaningful experience of being called by Jesus is necessary to this work. But it's not sufficient. As Methodists, we would hope for all Christians a meeting with the Lord Jesus would be assumed. But just as very few Christians should be allowed near the controls of an airplane or the scalpels in an operating room, so too should few be allowed near the number two job in a fast-growing church. The folks we interviewed bring extensive skills from the secular world to their jobs in the church. Lins and Sabra Engelbrecht of The Gathering in St. Louis are both trained as lawyers. Engelbrecht says that training does help her with human resource questions, building and zoning issues with the city, complicated contracts beyond what most private individuals have to sort through. Sisney is trained as a comedian (hold the jokes please). But she knows how to toggle between tasks quickly and efficiently: "From stocking the toilet paper to a five-figure purchase order." Lins started with plugging in cords and still has to come in on off days to take out the trash. This is a specialized sort of omnicompetence—one that knows how to get done *whatever* needs doing, including the lowliest tasks in the building. This is a sort of competence that reflects a Christ who was in the very nature of God, and also emptied himself. Service and grandeur are never opposed. They rather meet, and marry, in church.

Trust Is Everything

Competence is also necessary but not sufficient. Plenty of competent people wouldn't work out in this role. As important as raw ability is, trustworthiness is more important still. Being a pastor is a lonely job—even a pastor surrounded by thousands of people. As gifted as these lead pastors are, they need time and space to decompress, think out loud, unburden themselves, and kick around ideas in safety. Number twos have to know things that others in the church do not have to know (financial giving data for example). And they have to be absolutely trustworthy. One slip of confidential information and trust is smashed forever. These number twos treat their trusts with appropriate, well, trustworthiness. Engelbrecht calls herself an "external processor." She thinks aloud. Nevertheless, she knows more than anyone about the details of life at The Gathering, and often those details are sensitive and/or confidential. So she can't process aloud, can't say, why the one who talks in the meetings as though he gives a lot actually doesn't. (And lay reader, if you're wondering whether this is you, the answer is most definitely "yes.")

Matt Miofsky knows he can go into Sabra's office, close the door, and let his (quite metaphorical) hair down: He can't take this or that anymore. He can't stand *x* or *y*. Why on earth? He can vent this way because he knows Sabra won't "freak out," as she says. He also knows she'll take whatever he says to God and then to her grave. The number twos with whom we spoke agree on this—full and total trustworthiness is essential to the job. I (Jason) am so accustomed to seeing mainline parishes run badly, I had assumed basic competence was of the utmost importance to turn things around. It is, all agree. Yet as important as it is, full discretion and confidentiality are more important still. The desert fathers speak of the godliness of certain early Christian monks this way. They would hide the sins of their brethren. Not because sins don't matter—sins matter enough that people moved to the desert and gave up money, sex, and power to get rid of their sins. Sin matters greatly—but being godly and hiding sin, overlooking it, even *forgetting* it, matters more (Ps 103:12).

Trust extends to ways of communicating. Number twos have to know when to go to the number one and when not to. What requires attention from above and what does not? To misjudge is to run into the "swoop and poop" problem of the senior stepping in and undoing what's been done previously. This takes away the number two's agency and reduces trust that he or she will take things off the pastor's plate, not add to it. Engelbrecht speaks of the whole staff of The Gathering trusting her to know what to bring to Matt and how. It can be done wrong, as Scott Chrostek and Sisney both admit. In an early meeting, Sisney was being her outspoken self with an external constituent. Scott spoke up after her: "What Kelly is *trying* to say is..." Sisney fumed silently for the rest of the meeting until she got the chance to say to him later, "Don't ever do that to me again." Now they joke about the time when he *mansplained* for her—in fact,

"What Kelly's *trying* to say" has become a recurring punchline of the staff. (We seniors deal with so much crap from our staffs, don't we?!). Who says what, and to whom, is a delicate question and can involve hurt feelings. But the number two also brings gifts the pastor does not. Namely—folks can find them. Scott Chrostek tells often the story of putting thirty five pennies in each shirt pocket. Each time he invited someone to the church, he would switch a penny to the other pocket. He wouldn't go home until the pennies were all switched. Well, who was at the church office while Scott was playing pennies at every coffee shop in the River City? Kelly Sisney. She's who folks could find—and so she became a sort of second face for Resurrection Downtown. And of course, given the pastor and number two are working in close proximity over things that matter, feelings get hurt. We have to practice internally, as church, what we say works for all of humanity: forgiveness. Sisney speaks of having to say to Chrostek, "You're my friend, but what you did hurt me." The two can yell at one another down the hallway in a way that alarms other staff—but they're like siblings; they can take it. Engelbrecht speaks of the growing friendship between her and her husband and Miofsky and his wife. Lins jumped into the job pool for the executive post at Providence because he was Jacob's friend; he could see how the job of growing the church was wearing on him, and that Jacob needed help. Travis Waltner at Embrace in Sioux Falls says that Adam Weber's strength is also his area of growth: he pushes his staff to the moon. And he wants to get there yesterday. This can make for a crazy environment. It's also the identity of the church—a restlessness to reach the world. Yesterday if possible.

Methodism at its best is a tradition that encourages Christians to "watch over one another in love." The pastor and number two at these churches do precisely that. They care about one another's

souls, marriages, discipleship, and leadership—in something like that order.

Each of these folks started at the church as a worshiper before they worked for the place. Each was attracted to the church's vision for the kingdom of God, for human flourishing generally, for the blessing of the neighborhood. And each gave something up to jump in professionally. Each triages well, problem-solves with the best of them, presents problems to the pastor that are already solved, not just ones that are unsolvable (Lord knows there are enough of those). Each makes the pastor look good before the pastor even sees the problem coming. And each pastor is fully aware they couldn't do what they do without this person. So each continues to get promoted: Engelbrecht from director of operations to executive; Lins from cable plugger-inner to executive; Sisney from the host who welcomed the Chrosteks to Kansas City to the indispensable person at Resurrection Downtown; Waltner from a parishioner to chief administrator and then campus pastor. Each is like the queen on a chessboard to their pastor's king. It's tempting to say that the pastor could change more easily than the number two.

Who's the Next Timothy?

It is easy to look at some of these examples and throw one's hands up in the air. What if a church doesn't have the money for a second staff person, much less an executive pastor or number two? The virtue still applies. In talking with many of these churches, we found out that even in the beginning, before any people came or any dollars were given, these pastors were thinking in terms of alliances and partnerships. They were aware of what they could do well, and what they couldn't. They were less interested in doing everything

Eight Virtues of Rapidly Growing Churches

themselves and more interested in finding others who could come alongside them in leading. Oftentimes, number twos emerge as an especially engaged lay person, a ministry assistant, or a person who is willing to give an extra amount to a particular ministry. Number twos do not have to be paid staff; in fact they rarely are. As pastors, we have to look for number two types, whether we lead a small group of ten or a church of ten thousand.

We try to build this principle in at every level of The Gathering. In our CoreGroup ministry (small groups at The Gathering), every leader is asked to keep an eye out on a person in their group that has the gifts for leading. We encourage leaders to begin grooming that person, allow them to lead, ask them to send the weekly e-mails or lead prayers. At the end of every CoreGroup year, we ask each leader to name someone in their group who could possibly lead a new group. Occasionally a new leader emerges this way. But in every instance, a CoreGroup leader develops a number two who helps make the group work. They share the leadership burden and offer competencies that complement that of the leader. Whether you are a youth pastor over thirty kids, a Sunday school teacher with a class of ten, or a pastor of a church of 150—there is power in having a number two.

Number twos know enough to know they would not want to replace their boss. Pastoring is a lonely job. I (Jason) remember a study of university administrators that asked whether other employees of the school would want the president's job. Most said yes (imagining greater power and pay perhaps than is actual in that office). One person more consistently said no: those already in provost roles. That is, number twos see enough to know they don't want the number one position. They're in a role that exercises the best of their gifts for the indisputable good of the institution. They see the nonsense the leader has to take on for the sake of the whole. They get that the person in charge is never "off": their public role is 24/7. If something goes wrong, responsibility is not on the number two's head. As Spock says to Kirk in one *Star Trek* film: "If I may be so bold, it was a mistake for you to accept promotion." Kirk's best role was captain of the *Enterprise*, not admiral at a desk. And Spock's is as his first officer.

Or maybe, as the later *Star Trek: The Next Generation* put it, the first officer should actually be referred to as "Number One."

RAPIDLY GROWING CHURCHES PREACH WELL TO THE SKEPTIC

I f you listen to the pastors of these churches preach for any amount of time, you'll notice a few things quickly. One, they're really, really good. People don't turn up to church for lousy preaching. And lots of folks are turning up at these churches. Good preaching is necessary but not sufficient. Lots of good preachers blast away at empty pews. But it is necessary. Two, they're really, really good at speaking to non-church people. That is, they don't go on about insider churchy things. (Remember how awesome the bake sale is every year? See Betty to help . . .) They rather speak well to what we call their own "inner skeptic." That is, their imagined listener is not sure they buy this Christianity stuff. They're present Sunday under some duress and not altogether happy about it. There may be something more than what we can see and touch and hear—who these days isn't "spiritual but not religious"? But think of all the terrible things Christians have done in history. All the problems in the Bible and in faith. All the nut jobs who believe. All the preachers who make off with money. All the . . . . The skeptical mind is very busy.

The thing is, these preachers know that skeptical mind. In fact, they have one themselves. Olu Brown of Impact Church in Atlanta says simply, "Every time I preach, or do anything related to this vocation, I'm coming from that perspective: I'm the biggest doubter." I defy you to find a sentence in their preaching that hasn't passed through the skeptical filter. These folks know how they sound to outsiders, and they work that angle brilliantly. They don't do what's sometimes called in the church *apologetics*. That is, they don't directly bring up objections to faith and say why those objections are wrong or stupid. They don't go in for frontal assaults on listeners' doubt. Rather, they notice it. Honor it. Preach toward it. And they subtly find ways past, through, over, under, and around it. Pastors of rapidly growing churches preach well to the skeptic in the pew. Because they see a skeptic in the mirror in the morning when they brush their teeth.

Tilt Toward the Doubt

I don't mean by calling them "skeptics" to say that they don't believe. Of course they do. None of this would work if they didn't. The story is told of David Hume, the great eighteenth-century Scottish philosopher and famous critic of Christianity, learning his companion on the road is off to one of the revivals of George Whitefield, perhaps the greatest of the Methodist circuit riding evangelists. "Come on, you don't *believe* any of that stuff, do you?" The man on the way to the revival replied, "No, not really. But *he* does." The authenticity of Whitefield's faith itself bore witness. So it is with these preachers. They have a love for God that centers what they do, who they are, and is the most attractive thing about each of their preaching. But authenticity itself is not enough. Flat-earthers and alien abduction storytellers and Sasquatch watchers can be sincere. And that's where these preachers' genius kicks in. They know folks out there have reasons galore *not* to believe. They remember a time when they didn't. Or they can plausibly put themselves in the mind frame of someone who doesn't. Skeptics in their midst feel respected. Their doubts are engaged, not disdained. And often they stay, become believers, servants, leaders. Tim Keller gives the advice that if preachers preach as though there are non-Christians present, they will start showing up. If we do not, they will not. That is, the folks who casually come our way will notice if we, the preacher, have taken their doubts seriously. And they'll notice if we don't—and never turn back up. Church people will notice if they can bring their non-Christian friends or not. And this is not just for new people. Laura Heikes of Bee Creek Methodist outside Austin asks, "Don't a lot of people have doubts? Lots of believers have doubts and questions and concerns." And they are disarmed by preaching that knows this, doubts alongside, and finds reasons to believe all the same.

Jorge Acevedo of Grace Church in Florida preaches in lots of different voices. Some try to connect with a "felt need" in the culture. Some try to introduce hearers to a need they didn't know they had. But in all his preaching, he has a goal: "to tilt toward the skeptic and the person who does not yet believe." Acevedo brings up great spokespersons for the faith like N.T. Wright today and Blaise Pascal of seventeenth-century France. Wright speaks of the "echo of a voice," Pascal of a God-shaped vacuum—something in each of us that can surprise us by almost involuntarily responding, "That makes sense! Something inside me says that's the way to live." Acevedo imagines that if more of us preached that way, 85 percent of our congregations would not be declining, as they are.

This observation about speaking to our inner skeptic well may be even more particularly Methodist than others in this book. Methodism is nothing if not a revivalist sect. And if we're not reviving anybody—then what are we there for?! Anglicans were doing just fine at baptizing, eucharizing, marrying, and burying, carrying on the life of a parish without any thought to whether the souls of those turning up (or more often, not) were awakened to grace. These preachers know that the most beautiful thing happens when a person, who once did not believe in Jesus in any significant way, yet turns around, leaves behind a life without hope or God or thought of others, and becomes one with Christ. Such faith shows others around him or her that things are entirely different now, and that their life is spent focused on others. We Methodists preach for conversion. Or when we remember ourselves we do, anyway. These churches remember themselves. And they preach Jesus. And others come and are changed.

Prepare to Honor the Skeptic

Let's contrast this with a denomination (nameless) in the city where I (Jason) teach. A giant in pulpit ministry in this town had a reputation for thinking up what he was going to say *on the steps into the pulpit.* I was laughing about this with others from his denomination and was told, "No, that wasn't him, that was this other preacher. She thought up her sermons *during the procession.*" Same story, different character. Telling the story again to another gathering, I was corrected once more. "No, that was Bishop X. He thought up his sermons *while he was giving them.*" Historical Jesus scholars could go to work figuring out the origin of this story. But its widespread retelling, with the detail of who it's about moving around a bit, shows what the denomination thinks about sermon preparation: it's not important. If you're smart and accomplished you can speak off the top of your head.

I shudder to think what a congregation would get from me off the top of my head: the latest e-mail forward, my current political hobbyhorse, some undigested spiritual insight, all vaguely tied to the text I didn't bother to read before I read it aloud from the pulpit. And indeed that's what much of mainline preaching sounds like: rehashed preconceptions poorly delivered and not at all practiced. Is it any wonder folks don't turn up? We don't honor their presence with our preparation; we disappoint their nascent desire to hear a word from the Lord by offering our own ill-formed thought sludge.

By contrast these preachers are excellent. They'd be interesting to hear read from the phone book. Jacob Armstrong has a resonant, sweet, bass voice that makes me want to curl up in it and take a nap. Matt Miofsky has a kind of quirky genius—he's fascinated by whatever he's talking about, and soon you are too. Adam Weber has a kind of barely-contained-glee that burns hot in the pulpit but somehow doesn't boil over. Scott Chrostek has a nerdy enthusiasm over what he's saying that makes you lean in as a listener. Jorge Acevedo makes clear he's poured over some idea, wrestled it to the ground, and produced a hard-won blessing from it. Laura Heikes manages to talk about whatever she's describing as if it's the most interesting thing in the world—and you believe her. And Olu Brown could wring an "amen" from a floor ornament. Here's the point: with this many natural gifts *none of them has to work hard.* They could coast on talent for decades if they wanted. But they do work hard—tilting toward the skeptic. And you can tell. They preach through current controversial events in the church in the world (think: Ferguson, Missouri, after unrest there). They dive into controversial scriptural and ethical issues (not just homosexuality, but wealth and poverty and politics too). They name hardship in their parish. And they linger with the word of God until they have a word for their gathered

85

church. You can tell when someone has trembled in God's presence, sweated over the scripture, practiced in front of the mirror—and these preachers have. May their tribe increase.

For example, Adam Weber's church is named for the epiphany he had about scripture. "Embrace" is what the father does to his prodigal son on his return (Luke 15). Weber was a good, religious kid. Who isn't in South Dakota? But, he says, "I had heard about God my entire life, but I had never heard that God could name the brokenhearted, that God knows and loves them. I never knew that before a word is on our tongue God knows it completely. I never knew as Zephaniah says that God sings over us [Zeph 3:17]. I never knew any of that."

Weber knew about God. But he didn't *know* God. And he didn't realize how much difference that would make in his life. His associate, Travis Waltner, describes the way Weber *lives* to reach the next person for Christ (so much so he can make life hard on his staff!). Weber puts it this way, riffing off of another beloved parable of Jesus: "We have *one* value at Embrace: we will do anything and everything to reach the next person for Jesus. For most churches that's not true; they would never leave ninety-nine for the one, ever, ever, ever, honestly, ever." I think he means "ever."

One example of this "ever" is the plethora of empty buildings in Methodism. Miofsky relates that his evangelical church-planting friends lust after the opportunities that we Methodist church planters have. Because we have unused buildings. And we have the structure to take those buildings and give them to planting or replanting endeavors. Embrace has recently been handed one such empty building in Minnesota to start its first campus outside South Dakota. Several of Miofsky's and Resurrection's campuses are formerly family chapel Methodist buildings that could easily have been sold and become condos or nightclubs. Instead, they're places where the gospel is being preached in a culturally enticing way that's making new disciples for Jesus. We used to do that writ large in our movement, you know. Our Connexion was an evangelical enterprise. These places show it can be again.

Contemplate the Darkness

One reason, pious as it sounds to say it this way, is that life is awfully dark. Weber gave me two examples. One, he was standing outside his house one day and watched a mother stroll by with her baby, unnoticed. Beaucolic, right? But then something the child said or did set her off. She took off her shoe (hopefully a light one!), reared back, and threw it at her baby full force with everything she had. Weber wondered: What set her off like that? How was she hurt that she so wanted to hurt someone powerless—her precious child? Another example: Embrace doesn't have many funerals. Most of its growth is among young families, so they have the occasional miscarriage they lament, and the occasional suicide. The first adult funeral Weber did was of a young man he'd only been talking to *seven hours* before he heard of his suicide. Nothing seemed amiss. Yet clearly everything was amiss. "I'm not a fire and brimstone preacher," Weber says. "But every time I hear about a shooting or a suicide I wonder, 'Gosh, if I could have just introduced them to the Lord, would it have made any difference?'" Ever alert to his inner skeptic, he half-answers: "Maybe not. Even the best Christian people have done these things. But we are so lost without Jesus." In the church, we place such a high premium on niceness that we almost don't stop to notice how miserable and wretched life is for so many. Preaching that seems oblivious to the depths of despair afoot in our world will strike skeptics as disconnected, naïve, or worse—a lie. As I write, *13 Reasons Why* is a Netflix phenomenon about teen suicide while countless churches flirt with the prosperity gospel, sing happy-clappy music, and admit not an ounce of pain. But preaching that shows it's at least aware of the darkness might scratch out a hearing about light.

Scott Chrostek tells a story in his book *The Misfit Mission* of going on a mission trip to Appalachia.[1] Brenda from Kentucky had strangers from a church descend on her house to repair a roof and chimney. And that's not all. She got to telling them about her nine-year-old boy who was run over and killed by a fifteen-year-old in the community. The killer got a month in juvenile detention and is now free. Other preachers had told her that her boy was forever lost, for he'd never accepted Jesus. Not coincidentally Brenda was lost too. The team members started to talk of how Jesus heals. That he doesn't let any part of creation go. That his love isn't gauged only for those who say the correct religious formula. But that it's for those most brokenhearted. Like her. Like her boy. By the end, grace and mercy poured out in the room: "Sweaty, stinky strangers hugged it out in the middle of Appalachia."[2]

Now imagine how a skeptic might hear that story—there go Christians again, patting themselves on the back for "helping" while probably supporting barbaric politics that keep people poor. But they would also have to wonder—who turns down the cruise ship and goes to build houses in Appalachia on their spare time? Why? And the ranks of atheists comforting heartbroken strangers with whom they share nothing in common are rather thin. Granted, Chrostek's crew was undoing damage done *by other churches*. But the story is thick, rich, human, and might set doubter to wondering.

---

1. Scott Chrostek, *The Misfit Mission: How to Change the World with Surprises, Interruptions, and All the Wrong People* (Nashville: Abingdon Press, 2016).
2. Ibid., 141.

Chrostek describes the way he grew up outside of the church. His lifelong friends aren't church people—they're mostly not religious, working in fields like law, film, commercial real estate, and, he says, mostly Jewish. Scott knows how churchy church people sound to non-Christians. He knows how *not* to speak in such off-putting ways. Scott imagined himself on Wall Street and did work in investments for a while, making three hundred phone calls a day to find eight to ten potential clients ready to invest with him. When he writes of those times, you can tell his blood is pumping a little faster—he loved it and misses it. Yet now he hustles another way. He spends his time in coffee shops around Kansas City meeting people and getting to know them. The same hustling he once did for investors he now does for church. And it's worked: Resurrection Downtown is building one of the first grand new churches in an American inner city in decades. Scott's own zeal leave people wondering—what drives him like that?

Work Hard. Love Even Harder.

Aristotle would be impressed. He taught that we human beings *are* what we do regularly. Methodism has believed that too—so we have prescribed how to follow Jesus very precisely. And Scott is disciplined in his habits. What sounds exhausting to anyone even slightly more introverted (he has tips for how to talk people up in line at the coffee shop!) makes Scott more fully alive. Early Methodists would approve. We were disciplined about prayer, visiting the poor, preaching about Jesus. And it made more of us than we would have been on our own.

But this relentless focus on new people is not simply ceaseless hard work, self-generated. Augustine taught that human beings are what we love. That is, every true human desire is planted in us by

89

God, and meant to be met by God. "When you are out in the community with people and really listen to them, you learn all sorts of
things," Chrostek told us in an interview. "You learn what drives
them, what they long for, what they wrestle with—you listen and
that becomes part of what you want to address." And it informs
preaching: "This seems to be what folks are talking about, so let's
wrestle with that topic." Because Scott loves God, he honors the
people God longs to reach—by listening to them. This isn't a one-off
affair for Chrostek alone. He invites his church to neighbor with
him. In a recent sermon series, Resurrection designed tic-tac-toe
boards with eight squares around the middle square that represents
one's home. The goal was to encourage listeners to get to know the
folks in the eight homes immediately surrounding them. What are
their names? Their family members' names? What do they do? More
importantly than such small talk—what do they long for? Regret?
How can their Christian neighbors bless them, be blessed by them?
We see a glimpse of the intellectual life of these churches—Jay Pathak
and Dave Runyon's *The Art of Neighboring* was new at the time, and
Resurrection Downtown just instituted it. And here Chrostek and
Resurrection have identified the loneliness at the heart of how we
live, and invited the church to join with God in doing something
about it, on the way to making their city better.

Scott mentions apologetics more positively in *The Misfit Mission*.
He wants to equip his fellow church members at Resurrection to
have an answer for the hope that is in them, as he does (1 Pet 3:15).
So they read books together by Resurrection founder Adam Hamilton or by America's greatest urban church planter, Tim Keller. He's
clear apologetics doesn't mean apologizing-for! It means showing
the faith in the clearest possible light, in a way that will be compelling for those listening. But I'm struck that Chrostek doesn't preach

in a defensive manner, explaining away weaknesses, hammering on strengths, as some apologists do. He just tells the stories of Jesus. That is, he meets doubts and uncertainties enough to usher folks into his talking about Jesus from the Bible. It sounds simple, but as a professor of preaching let me tell you how hard that is to do. One small example—how long the lengths of time are in scripture. In John 5 Jesus heals a man who had been crippled for thirty-eight years. Chrostek contextualizes—thirty-eight years ago he wasn't alive, Elvis was king of rock, and Carter was in the White House. What a long time to suffer! In another sermon he contextualizes the woman who had been hemorrhaging for twelve years (Mark 5). He asks a room of folks still celebrating the Kansas City Royals' World Series title in 2015, "Do you remember who the Royals' starting pitchers were twelve years ago? No? Exactly." And we're led to marvel at Jesus healing a shame so deep and so elusive of normal means of healing that he might even be able to heal us. And our enemies. Notice the point isn't to defend the historicity of the stories, though I'm sure Chrostek would have something to say about that if asked after. It's not to insist that miracles happen or that people are going to hell without believing they do. It's to put us into the story. We're the ones crippled, marginalized, excluded. Jesus grabs us by the hand, fully aware of our agony, and makes us whole. Like he'll do with all creation.

As a church grows, our preaching as if "we remember what it is like not to believe..." does all sorts of things. It establishes credibility with outsiders, it puts at ease insiders who are going through periods of doubt, it speaks to teenagers who are going through, well, teenage years. It is also an act of pastoral care. Instead of fighting or arguing or apologizing, I acknowledge the difficulty of belief with you, and in preaching we explore that together. Instead of an attitude of "let me tell you why you are wrong" or "let me defend scripture," it is more an attitude of "I have that same doubt too, let's see if we can't figure this out together." There is something really powerful about a preacher that invites your doubts, shares them, uses them in the message, and then leads you on an adventure toward figuring some of them out. Matt asks preaching students to describe grace in two minutes without using any religious words. These exercises are very practical, very difficult, and they reveal something of the "genius" of these preachers. They are really, really good at these exercises! You won't catch these preachers using a word like "sanctification" without unpacking it. And when they unpack it, a church enters a mystery with them.

Miofsky also remembers a time when the church was not overly important to him. He'd had a Catholic upbringing of sorts and respected faith; it just didn't seem to matter much. A key mentor whom he admired and who had taken notice of him helped change that. But Miofsky remembers when insider church lingo repelled him too. So he doesn't use it.

Blandness Doesn't Conquer Skepticism

Some decades ago when "seeker-sensitive" churches were the growth program de jure, authors such as Rick Warren counseled us to grow churches big by avoiding controversy. We should also avoid weird religious symbols and obscure rituals, they advised. Regular Joes and Janes in Southern California and suburban Chicago wanted their faith like they wanted their shopping malls—pleasant, not too demanding, always offering a bargain in return for their time and money. This new generation of churches look different. They take their specs more from Keller and his heady engagement with New York City sophisticates—whom he often challenges in his preaching. Mark Driscoll, before his life blew up at Mars Hill in Seattle, preached like the movie *Fight Club*— he punched people in the face, and they came back and brought friends. Nadia Bolz-Weber in Denver is using her foul-mouthed cultural criticism and her nearly medieval mysticism to attract very non-traditional churchgoers. In other words, churches are becoming more pugnacious rather than bland, eschewing churchiness in order to highlight Jesus, asking for costly conversion, engaging the world in ways that make it uncomfortable, and showing listeners how odd Christians ought to be.

Miofsky, for example, was in the middle of a cultural firestorm in 2014 with the murder of Michael Brown and as civic unrest in Ferguson, Missouri, splayed across the world stage. A comfortable approach would be to shield his church from all the unpleasantness, trying to make the church into a refuge and sanctuary from the storm. Instead Matt and The Gathering ran toward the noise. He invited voices from Ferguson into his pulpit. He preached on race and white privilege in a way designed to make white people uncomfortable, to even make us, in the old revivalist language, repent. A certain blend of evangelicalism would soft peddle the issue if addressed at all, out of a sense that our primary concern is to introduce people to Jesus. But Miofsky knows meeting Jesus means learning to love all his weird friends. "To connect with folks right now who are skeptical, far from pushing aside controversy, we need to raise it up," he says. "That's part of being evangelical—keeping things weird." Christianity has been charged with being an opiate for the masses long before Marx coined that language. Skeptics of all kinds suspect us of this—because it has so often been true. But it doesn't have to be. Here Miofsky's preaching is functioning more like what William Barber, head of the North Carolina NAACP, calls a "moral defibrillator," shocking the body's heart till it beats with God's heart.[3]

Who's Talking up There?

Listening to Jacob Armstrong could drive a jealous preacher to despair. His voice is beautiful, strong, and resonant. He could hire himself out to read novels for publishing houses if this whole preaching thing doesn't work out. His voice has *welcome* in it, as if one can tell he has prayed before speaking. He does what all these preachers do well: "I'm Jacob, one of the pastors here." As if they aren't there for him. He, and the the other preachers in this book, assume they're not. They aren't prima donnas. In the church world, growing a big congregation is the brass ring. These preachers could write their ticket, increase their salary every year, drown out criticism, stop doing anything they don't want to do. An evangelical researcher, Michael Lindsay, who has interviewed all sorts of people told me the hardest people on the planet to interview are Hollywood stars and megachurch pastors—and for the same reason. Both have nothing to gain and everything to lose.[4] There's a reason people on pedestals become less human—we've asked them to be by our adulation. In any case Armstrong doesn't show the marks of this debilitating illness. For example, he shares details of dropping his girls off for their first day of school. He makes it all the way home before he "ugly cries." "These moments are precious," he counsels like a much older

---

3. See: https://www.washingtonpost.com/news/acts-of-faith/wp/2017/06/29/woe-unto
-those-who-legislate-evil-rev-william-barber-builds-a-moral-movement/?utm_term=.b7ce
faa43a26.

4. For further insight, see D. Michael Lindsey, *Faith in the Halls of Power* (Oxford University Press, 2008).

man. In his book *The New Adaptors* he writes that the church's work has to be good news for the poor.[5] In Mt. Juliet, Providence Church heard about hundreds of homeless students in their community, and they mobilized to meet that need. This isn't just doing what Jesus commands, though it is that. It's disarming to skeptics. Suddenly the doubter in us that says the church is just after our money notices they're actually doing something about this problem in town everybody else just laments. They're making our whole community better. This isn't the selfish me-first faith we all know to lampoon. It looks alarmingly like Jesus.

The first best thing Armstrong does is that introduction: "*One of* the pastors here." To introduce oneself seems embarrassingly obvious. But as I write this, I remember I failed to do it *last Sunday*. I get invited to preach occasionally at Tenth Church, the multisite megachurch congregation my wife used to serve in Vancouver. Last Sunday I just launched in, with no consideration for those who've never been there or have no idea who I am or why I'm talking to them. "Could you introduce yourself?" a site pastor asked before the fifth service. Too bad for those in services one through four. The "one of the" is key. As important as the founding pastor is, he or she can't speak as though they are.

Armstrong spent a recent sermon showing that he both is and isn't the key to Providence's story. A recent sermon series is called "Fixer Upper," on the book of Nehemiah and drawing on the popular "reality" show, arguing that all of us need renovation. Armstrong gives testimony that he's chief among those in need of repair. He tells his congregation often of a struggle with anxiety that saw him unable to sleep, driving aimlessly, even checking himself into the hospital.

---

5. Jacob Armstrong, with Adam Hamilton and Mike Slaughter, *The New Adapters: Shaping Ideas to Fit Your Congregation* (Nashville: Abingdon Press, 2015).

"I was so unsure what to do until I reached out and asked for help." His parents helped him, and he has his anxiety under control. "I go to the hospital a lot now," he says, as any pastor does. "But I never go there alone." The gospel is that we don't have to live disconnected lives. Here Armstrong differs markedly from those who preach that Jesus solves all of the problems in our individual lives. No—the problems don't vanish. But we don't have to face them alone. The cumulative effect of such stories is clear—Providence isn't about Jacob Armstrong. And contrary to what I said above, he doesn't discourage preacher-listeners, driving us to jealousy. Providence, like the church in general, is about Jesus's effort to family all of us. Methodists should know that above all.

"I'm convinced that church statisticians should all lose their jobs," Adam Weber says. When Embrace hit three thousand people, denominational bean counters rejoiced. What was God's response? "Well done," Weber snarks. "It took you eight years to do what my Spirit did at Pentecost with one sermon." His point is that we think too small and congratulate ourselves too quickly. Perhaps we can be forgiven. Though we're a revivalist sect we haven't been reviving many people lately. These instances of counter-example are indeed inspiring. If Weber and friends have their way, they won't just be that. They'll be not nearly enough, with a lot more to follow.

RAPIDLY GROWING CHURCHES MAKE FRIENDS WITH THE DENOMINATION

Rapidly growing churches make allies within their denomination, focusing on the strengths of working within a system.

There is a pastime among pastors who are doing innovative work: complaining about the boneheads in the denominational office who don't get it. We are both elders in The United Methodist Church and all of our examples are pulled from that denomination, but what we have to say applies to any denominational structure in which you find yourself. One of the most frustrating aspects of starting a new church, launching an innovative ministry, or pursuing a risky ministry initiative is navigating the labyrinthine bureaucratic processes for doing something new. If United Methodism's goal is to frustrate entrepreneurial leaders and suffocate creative ideas before they get off the ground, we are winning big. Now if you are a lover of the denomination, or even better, a judicatory official, stick with me. This chapter isn't going to be denomination bashing. But we have to name this reality, one that many pastors on the ground experience.

Alongside this reality there is another that is as equally unhelpful. We have all witnessed the new church start pastor who derides the system, complains about the processes, and assumes the system is only there to curtail their ground-breaking new models for ministry. They often lament the system, imagining that without the limitations, they would grow the next Resurrection. It is easy to lay every challenge and blame every miscalculation on the "system" that won't move fast enough, won't think creatively enough, or doesn't understand the way culture is changing. If the company men (and women) up at headquarters would just wake up, then maybe we could get the kind of encouragement and support we need out here. Oftentimes, it seems that these pastors want money, freedom, and autonomy without any of the accountability. I have personally witnessed young, passionate, and creative pastors assume that the denomination is there to make their life harder. More often than not, this is a self-fulfilling prophecy.

Help the System Help You

In the midst of these two extremes, the leaders of rapidly growing churches have an amazing ability to mitigate the limitations and obstacles that a system naturally creates while at the same time taking advantage of the benefits the system has to offer. All the while, these leaders actually seek to help and aid the denomination, and usually earn the respect of the denominational leaders in the process. The idea that the creative pastor has to be a maverick who butts heads with the powers that be is a myth. Leaders of rapidly growing churches collaborate with their denominational leaders in ways that limit frustration and mutually benefit both parties. Working this way not only is more effective, and earns such pastors more freedom, but also is a more enjoyable way to work.

For example, Jorge Acevedo talks about the wisdom of learning to lead up. Early in the life of Grace Church, Jorge knew that he wanted to pursue a model of multisite ministry that might challenge the status quo and raise the ire of conference watchdogs. Rather than fight with those who might question each new idea, he decided to invest in the district and conference in an effort to form relationships and help contribute to the overall efforts of the denomination. Far from pulling back from conference events as so many do, he began going to every district and conference event he could. He serves when and where it is feasible, and works to make himself available to the larger denomination. This has continued even up to the present time when he agreed to serve on The United Methodist Church's Commission on a Way Forward. By investing in the larger denomination, Jorge was able to earn the trust of the denominational leaders. These relationships helped him navigate the system when and where he needed to and created a positive backdrop against which he could try creative things. Jorge is able to "lead up" by investing in the system that in return supports him. Jorge is able to challenge the system, try new ideas, and garner resources in a much better way because of the time he has given and the positive relationships he has created.

We were surprised to find that in the case of most rapidly growing churches, the relationship between the local church leaders and conference leadership was marked by collaboration and mutual support more than acrimony and frustration. That isn't to say starting something new or leading something innovative doesn't come with frustrating roadblocks from the denominational system. Rather it means that the pastors of rapidly growing churches have figured out how to navigate the challenges while receiving the gifts that a denomination has to offer.

So what are those gifts and why is it worth it from the standpoint of an innovative leader to stay connected to a denomination? Years ago, as The Gathering was beginning to launch a second site, I (Matt) was talking to a pastor friend who leads a nondenominational church. While I don't remember the specifics, I was complaining about some denominational hoop that I had to jump through. He listened patiently and when I was done, he laid into me. I was surprised, for I had been expecting him to commiserate with me. Instead, he said to me, "I don't think you realize what you have. Do you know how many pastors would kill to have what you have in The United Methodist Church? Never mind money, support, and processes that help church planters—you have thousands of buildings! For pastors who want to go multisite, United Methodism is sitting on the single greatest resource that many church planters lack—buildings, located all over the place! You need to see the gift you have in the system you are in."

His words have always stuck with me. He was right of course. There may be some frustrations working in a denomination, but there are a lot of gifts. What we noticed from talking with the pastors of rapidly growing churches is that they are able to see through the frustrations to the gifts, and use those gifts in order to advance the mission of their church. It is easy to critique a denomination like The United Methodist Church, especially when it comes to innovation and creativity. But right now in our denomination and several others, there are a lot of gifts that entrepreneurial pastors would be wise to consider.

They'll Send You Checks. Really.

First, denominations have resources. Most conferences in The United Methodist Church have funding each year for new churches and revitalization efforts in existing churches. They are looking to fund thoughtful and creative work. Do you know how many leaders have good ideas but no way to pay for them? This funding comes with strings attached, and it should. They are using this money to invest in ministries that will further their mission. As people looking to take advantage of these opportunities, leaders have to understand that there will be some accountability. At times, this accountability may seem arbitrary; we may disagree with the benchmarks or criteria. We may complain about the fact that we have to fill out paperwork, attend a meeting, or fulfill a mandatory requirement. But in the end, denominations can help with one of the first and greatest challenges in doing creative work: funding. If one can accept some of the guidelines and accountability measures, recognizing that there is something fair about those funding an idea desiring to make sure the idea is working, then the denomination can be a huge ally to innovative work in a congregation.

Over the course of ten years at The Gathering, we have received four different grants, helping us to fund and start each of our four sites. Far from seeing the oversight as burdensome, we have learned to collaborate and see the denominational expectations as fair and healthy. The more we learn to collaborate with our conference, the more they have grown to trust us to use resources wisely. Over time, they have given us more latitude as we begin new ministries. Have I been frustrated by some of the requirements? Absolutely. But I can say this: I was much more frustrated early on. As we have learned to work together, and grown to trust the intentions of one another, I have a great relationship with the conference leaders in Missouri. Far from being an obstacle, our conference leadership has helped The Gathering to be what it is today. I am convinced that we would be a far weaker church without them, and I think that the Missouri

Conference is a better conference because of us. I coach other new start pastors all the time to see the benefits of the denomination. When it is possible, collaboration always works out better than acrimony.

But funding isn't the only benefit to working within a denomination. Along with money, most conferences in The United Methodist Church also have other resources for those looking to do new ministry. They have continuing education money, subscriptions to demographic services, easy ways to connect with others doing similar work, and wisdom about lessons learned in other places. When a church gets to a point of needing to hire staff, the connection provides a network for recruiting staff and local church leaders. None of this comes without frustrations. Those frustrations are real, and in many cases, stifling. But if a leader can find a way to mitigate frustrations, lead up, and collaborate with denominational leaders, there are huge benefits to being part of a large organization.

Bureaucrats: Clear Space, Pray, Encourage

Rapidly growing churches can teach pastors and local church leaders about the benefits of collaborating, but they also can teach judicatory officials as well. Each church we talked with had leaders who felt as if their bishop and conference staff were the exception to the general rule that The United Methodist Church system is set up to stifle creativity, not encourage it. Conference leaders who want new ministries to thrive in their area can learn from this. Without naming names, we talk with pastors all the time who experience conference staff that are more interested in making sure the i's are dotted and t's are crossed than they are in supporting creative ministry. As one pastor put it, "It's strange that we can agree to disagree on various interpretations of scripture, but we become fundamentalists when it comes to the *Book of Discipline*." The observation has merit. There are conferences where the leadership is so cautious to be sure that every element of the *Discipline* is followed that they snuff out a good idea before it ever sees the light of day. On the other hand, there are conferences led by bishops who see their job as clearing obstacles and nurturing creative ministry so that it can take root. As one bishop put it, "There is enough ambiguity in the *Book of Discipline* that whenever possible, I try to interpret it in a way that frees pastors up to do creative work." This mind-set among judicatory leaders seems to be a key ingredient in fostering rapidly growing congregations. Every pastor with whom we talked named their bishops and conference staff as allies and supporters in their growth.

For example, Laura Heikes points out that her conference, the Rio Grande, heard her request to be someplace Spanish-speaking in the Rio Grande Valley and decided instead to put her in far west Texas. But that church needed her, she grew in her skills, and she was ready to plant afterward. Likewise, Bee Creek wouldn't have asked for a woman for their second pastor. But they got her, and are thrilled. "That's the beauty of a connectional system. Appointments are filled with prayer, so even if they're not what we expect, I tend to trust the denomination."[1] Often innovative pastors leave and the congregation disintegrates soon thereafter, unaware of the supports they once had that would have held things in place. "We're glad to be part of the denomination," Laura said. "My church tends to say 'they gave us the money to start, sent us good pastors, so we're in debt to help others start too.'"

---

1. We Methodists are unusual in our practice of having bishops appoint preachers to churches. We are not shilling for this particular form of polity, just pointing out that a denomination's oddities should be viewed as assets.

It is worth considering more specifically what felt like "support" for a local church leader trying to do innovative work. In addition to concrete resources like money and buildings, there are often more subtle ways of supporting pastors. First, new ministries need protection when they are young. This is the stage when ideas are still fragile, haven't yet grown deep roots, and are often fumbling through trial and error to forge a strategy and identity. We cannot expect brand-new ministries to look like fully mature ones. During this early period, it is easy for other pastors and conference leaders to want to help, offer advice, and intervene when they see something that they believe will not work. This is easy to do since usually ministries at this stage are more dependent on funding, have young or new leaders, and may have a more difficult time being clear about what is helpful and what is not. District superintendents, congregational development staff, and even bishops can help by giving a new church or ministry time and space to figure it out, by running interference when others want to say, "I told you so." Research and development shouldn't be micromanaged, and it takes time. A leader may be trying something that you think is absolutely the wrong approach, but give new ideas some space. Most innovative things look stupid when they are first articulated. Most importantly, such leaders can reduce the circle of people who get an open venue to offer their perspective and advice. We may think it is helpful, but it usually isn't. When I started The Gathering, I got inundated with unsolicited advice. It can cause a new pastor to second-guess, question, and potentially even back off the more creative aspects of their new ministry.

Secondly, we have to allow new churches and ministries to "act their age." That means we have to develop metrics and criteria for progress that make sense to something new. To take a new church and after six months expect it to look like a fifty-year-old church isn't realistic. It isn't going to have a youth group, fully functioning kids' ministry, Wednesday night dinner, Sunday school classes, and a full committee structure. Don't expect it to. Instead, develop metrics that are realistic, make sense for its age, and measure things that are consistent with the mission and vision of the church. If the conference evaluation template doesn't fit the new church, throw away the freaking template, get out your laptop, and write a new one. Don't try to squeeze the new thing into the system that has been created for fully mature churches. Or dying ones.

Thirdly, learn to work with innovative people. They operate a bit differently. This isn't to say that they shouldn't follow the rules or be expected to conform to clergy expectations. It does mean that there are some quirks and personality traits that you can either react negatively to or learn to channel, shape, and help mature. I (Matt) will out myself on this one. As a young pastor, I had several faults. I was arrogant, thought I knew more than I did, was overly critical of the greater church, was occasionally rash, always opinionated, and impatient, to name just a few vices. I also had passion and some good ideas. I was willing to work more hours than almost anyone I knew, and I deeply, deeply wanted to share the gospel with as many new people as I could. I had a district superintendent who was a genius at figuring out how to lead me. She easily could have focused on my negatives and used them to put me in my place, and I would have deserved it. She didn't. Instead, she focused on my positives, channeled them and gave them better shape, opened up opportunities, and patiently worked with me as I matured and grew up. She was wise and humble, strong and loving, patient and persistent as she guided me and the new church that I was leading. I wouldn't be in ministry without her. But she knew how to work with me, and was willing to do things a bit differently with me in order to nurture something new and creative.

Let me be blunt. Creative people can be a pain. They aren't like you and that is a good thing. Creative people need to learn to collaborate well with the system, but conference leaders can also meet them halfway, learning how to better adapt systems and processes to give creative ministries and those that lead them some space to mature and develop.

Rapidly growing churches have leaders who have learned to mitigate the frustrations of denominational structure while benefiting from the gifts that such structures have. They navigate the sometimes arbitrary processes while investing in the greater denomination and forming relationships with those in conference leadership. They seek to collaborate rather than battle, and as a result, they are able to use the benefits and resources of the denomination for further growth. Denominational leaders who are charged with overseeing these churches overwhelmingly were willing to be flexible, adaptable, and patient in their leadership. They worked intentionally to create space where innovation could flourish and gave new ideas the benefit of the doubt whenever possible. This collaboration increases the likelihood that innovative ministry can take off in a particular place.

CONCLUSION

HOW TO PASTOR
LIKE A PLANTER

A s an author of this book, the best part of the process was interviewing other pastors. I (Matt) found that as I talked and learned from some of these rapidly growing churches, I was convicted, challenged, and inspired. Evaluating my own ministry is never easy. It is typically more convenient for me to assume everything is great unless someone comes to me with a problem. I often don't want to ask too many questions for fear that I might find ministries that are weaker or less effective than I imagine. But despite these temptations, having healthy conversation about how we are doing at our church has been instrumental to The Gathering's improvement and growth. Having a set of principles, values, or virtues to regularly talk about has been helpful. The 8 virtues have given us a way to regularly have conversations about the health of our ministry.

The virtues discussed in this book are likely not new to many of you; most of them weren't new to me. As a pastor, I *know* these virtues are important, and I *intend* to champion them at my church. I also know that over time these virtues slip in importance or attention. Pastoral work often feels like a game of whack-a-mole: just as soon as we deal with one problem, another pops up. Pretty soon, a year or two goes by, and we realize that a virtue we once talked about

107

a lot has gotten little recent attention. Maybe our strategy has grown stale or our approach is becoming dated. Maybe we've had a lot of good ideas but have never gotten around to executing them. Perhaps we used to be known for one of these virtues, but over time our focus has drifted. All of these have been true for various virtues at my own church. Whatever the reason, revisiting these virtues has been a refreshing and revitalizing exercise for our church and many others around the country.

So what should you do with these virtues? Let me offer a couple of suggestions. At The Gathering, we practice a very simple exercise to evaluate how we are doing. When we want to evaluate a certain area of ministry, I gather a group of staff or lay ministry leaders around a table. (Maybe for your ministry this would consist of a church board, a leadership team, or a group of key volunteers.). Then we take a virtue and ask two questions: "How are we doing?" and "Which direction are we headed?" For the first question, I ask them to give me a green, yellow, or red light. *Green* means we are doing great in this area. *Red* means we have neglected this area or it needs serious attention. *Yellow* is somewhere in the middle (and we try to use yellow sparingly). For the second question, I ask them to give me an up arrow, down arrow, or neutral line. The *up arrow* means we are currently getting better. The *down arrow* means we are losing momentum or effectiveness. The *neutral* response means we are treading water but not improving.

I have consistently taken time to check in with my team on how we are doing with each one of these virtues. The conversations are challenging, revealing, and productive. The dialogue allows people to say things that sometimes they have been reluctant to say. The evaluation not only reveals strengths and weaknesses, but more importantly, where we are currently improving and where we are neglecting a virtue. There are a few situations that warrant further attention. It is important to pay attention to those green light areas that also have a down arrow. We might be doing well now, but perhaps we have become complacent or have taken our foot off the gas. I also want to identify any red areas that have an up arrow. That means we have recognized the problem and are working on a solution.

The key to this evaluative work for my church is that we don't just do it once, but we regularly revisit and reevaluate. At The Gathering, we are changing rapidly, so I prefer to do it a bit more often, maybe a couple of times a year. Depending on your setting, maybe this is more of an annual exercise. Regardless of your context, when you do the exercise repeatedly, you get to see how you are changing and improving over time. It helps leaders to know where you are putting your focus and resources and why. Most of all, it has helped us rally around a virtue and get better at it.

As I have shared these virtues with pastors and leaders in churches of all sizes, the most common piece of feedback I receive is that they are practical and immediately relevant. Leaders can take these virtues to their church board or staff and immediately have a set of conversations that help them focus on how they are doing and where they can put future resources or attention. A lot of pastors have used the virtues in a series of meetings, perhaps dedicating each week to a conversation about a different virtue. Some boards have taken a half-day retreat to talk about all 8 of them at once. My hope is that the virtues can be revisited so that churches can evaluate how they are doing over time.

We have designed the virtues so they identify important areas of ministry or raise significant questions, while at the same time leaving space for your church to figure out what this virtue needs to look like in your setting. Teaching and practicing generosity is important, for example. But, your approach to living out that virtue is going to be different than my way. The solutions aren't as important as the questions and conversations. Our hope is that these virtues have not only helped you to understand some of the common attributes of churches that have grown rapidly, but more importantly, given you a set of questions and conversations that can propel your own ministry forward.

Made in the USA
Middletown, DE
06 December 2019